BEYOND GREED

to Charlie
best wishes

BEYOND GREED

A TRADITIONAL CONSERVATIVE
CONFRONTS
NEOCONSERVATIVE EXCESS

HUGH
SEGAL

FOREWORD BY PETER LOUGHEED

Stoddart

Published by Stoddart Publishing Co. Limited
34 Lesmill Road, Toronto, Canada M3B 2T6

Distributed in Canada by General Distribution Services Inc.,
34 Lesmill Road, Toronto, Canada M3B 2T6.
Tel. (416) 445-3333; fax (416) 445-5967;
e-mail Customer.Service@ccmailgw.genpub.com

01 00 99 98 1 2 3 4 5

Canadian Cataloguing in Publication Data
available from the
National Library of Canada.

ISBN 0-7737-3053-2

Jacket Design: Bill Douglas @ The Bang
Text Design: Kinetics Design & Illustration
Printed and bound in Canada

We gratefully acknowledge the Canada Council for the Arts and the Ontario Arts Council for their support of our publishing program.

To the Right Honourable Robert Lorne Stanfield, from whom I learned the fundamental conservative truth that there is no contradiction between the values of compassion, freedom, social responsibility, frugality, and enterprise — and that to suggest otherwise was to diminsh the very utility of modern conservatism to the public at large. He was truly the very best prime minister Canada never had.

Contents

Foreword

It was the Right Honourable John Diefenbaker who was quoted as saying, "If everyone thought the same way, no one would be thinking . . ." It is in that spirit of open debate and wide-ranging thought that I embrace the idea of this invigorating book without necessarily agreeing with everything in it.

Conservatism has always been a movement, an idea set in transition — distinguishable from doctrinaire socialism by the absence of rigid or limiting ideology. Certainly most parts of Canada have their own conservative tradition, and conservatism at the national level has always been enriched by that diversity.

My own experience in this diversity may be a useful prelude to this book.

When I decided in the mid-1960s to commence a career in elective politics, my original intentions were directed towards federal politics, which was normal for a young person. However, it was suggested by some friends that I pursue provincial politics as the leader of the Alberta Progressive Conservative party, which had no seats and had never formed the provincial government. I rather quickly demurred!

The province at the time was under the administration of the Social Credit party and the premier was Ernest Manning. It was the general consensus that Social Credit ran an honest and straightforward administration, by and large. It was fiscally responsible and regulated the oil and gas industry in an efficient manner.

However, a second look caused me to change my mind. Upon closer examination, Social Credit seemed to be quite authoritarian in their practices, exclusionary rather than inclusive in terms of participation, and very isolationist in attitude insofar as the mainstream of Canadian life was concerned.

So I decided to challenge Social Credit and out of this experience I began to articulate my own political philosophy. As a pragmatist, I tended to be flexible and not rigid. Although generally a free enterpriser on economic issues, I was very much the *Progressive* Conservative on social issues. Our first bill after we were elected in 1971 was a strong Bill of Rights and our second was the repeal of the odious Social Credit Sexual Sterilization Act.

Through my twenty years of elective political life, I often paused to reflect on my Progressive Conservative philosophy. What did I believe in and why did I do so?

Some of my strong views included much more inclusion of all points of view in the party and also in the caucus. Also, more open and contested democratic nomination meetings. As well, definitely more sensitivity towards the changing racial and multicultural Alberta that was evolving.

At the same time, I observed with great interest the evolution of the federal Progressive Conservative party through the leadership phases of John Diefenbaker, Bob Stanfield, Joe Clark, Brian Mulroney, Kim Campbell, and Jean Charest.

I now observe the current challenges to the more progressive traditions of the party in national politics. Conservatism is always a movable debate about the way in which the most important values at the root of a free society should be applied and about the purpose of society overall.

Thus I was delighted to read this work by Hugh

Segal. It could not be more timely or more relevant. It is a must read for those who care about political thought and political will.

I need not agree with all of the author's ideas to warmly applaud the debate this book will produce. We need the debate encouraged by this effort. For conservatives who seek a framework for tomorrow, this book not only asks the right questions but it raises some valuable answers.

Mr. Segal's book emphasizes as most do the identification of the right and left on the political spectrum. I do not think politically in these terms, but I accept the reality that it is the common usage and parlance. For me, I found that on most issues the key principle was the pull between the place of the individual in our society and the often conflicting need to respond to the requirements of the community at large. But where Hugh Segal and I come together is on the issue of rights *and* responsibilities.

Years ago on the Canadian pavilion at Expo '67 in Montreal was inscribed the phrase "Rights Are the Rewards of Responsibility." This has always been my basic and fundamental belief — that those who seek to claim rights can only make such claim if they themselves have been responsible to society as a whole.

The significance of this line of thinking appears

time and again through Hugh Segal's penetrating views of the contemporary Canadian political scene.

Certainly I applaud the call by Mr. Segal for a politics of humanity and civility — and his emphasis on the importance of community in the value structure of society. And, I agree wholeheartedly that isolationism or ethnocentricity — any effort to cut off Canadian society from the pluralism and the global view the new world requires — is both wrongheaded and economically of great potential disaster.

My home is Calgary, my province is Alberta, my country is Canada. But the place I do business and where more and more Canadian companies, universities, governments, and individuals will have to compete is the world itself. The core ideas that must govern how we organize ourselves as a free society will matter more and more every day. From Hong Kong to Istanbul, Cape Town to Prague, Riyadh to St. Petersburg, Canadians will be competing for a share of the new economic reality that will be essential to sustaining our quality of life at home. It would be a shame if the three major forces of democratic socialism, liberalism, and conservatism were detached from the need to evolve along with other Canadian institutions to address that central reality. The organizing premises of how we govern ourselves will matter. Conservatives should be the very last to shy from this debate.

Beyond Greed engages the debate head on with a candor, focus, and reason that is attractive. Having known Hugh Segal for about twenty-five years, I have never failed to enjoy his articulate defence even of ideas and policies with which I could not, as an Albertan, ever agree.

This book invites Conservatives everywhere to pause a moment and reflect on the kind of conservatism we want in the competitive political mainstream. In invites even those on the more conservative end of the conservative spectrum to think and reflect.

Mr. Diefenbaker's nostrum has always been relevant but never more than today, especially for conservatism. On economic, social, and unity issues, the cost of narrow-mindedness everywhere on the spectrum would be very high indeed.

Beyond Greed makes many points not all on the conservative spectrum will agree with. But its core intellectual thrust is to advocate precisely against a narrowing of minds or limiting of debate. Mr. Diefenbaker would agree very much with this approach. My own Alberta-based Progressive Conservatism could not be more comfortable with its purposes.

The debate begun in this book is about what conservatives should and could be. That debate has never mattered more. I am delighted to see Hugh Segal tackle it. It is an important and helpful contribution to a discussion that is vital not only to Conservatives but to democrats everywhere.

PETER LOUGHEED
CALGARY

Acknowledgments

The challenge of identifying the excesses of neo-conservatism emerged as a natural evolution from the moderate conservative models that shaped my own political views.

Among my fellow conservatives, I have taken great courage from the way in which two very different conservatives, former premier Bill Davis of Ontario and former premier Peter Lougheed of Alberta, have steadfastly defended their own different yet essentially moderate brands of conservatism — never losing the courage to be Progressive Conservatives appropriate to their time and place. The decency, pragmatism, and serious concern about society as a whole that Bob

Stanfield brought to every aspect of his public life, both as premier of Nova Scotia and national Conservative leader, have always been the most compelling of guiding lights for me in the public policy process.

At the School of Policy Studies at Queen's University in Kingston, numerous discussions with Keith Banting, the school's director, Tom Courchene, Bob Wolfe, Tom Williams, Tom Kent, Lisa Powell, Lynn Freeman, Patrick Fafard, and Sam Davis have helped me develop the argument for a more civil conservatism. While we spoke about many different public policy issues, and these colleagues are all more learned than I am and quite likely to my right or left on the political spectrum, their varied perspectives and thoughful expertise are an endless source of creative crosscurrents from which ideas and the odd insight emerge.

One friend who was particularly encouraging and thoughtful on the issues addressed in this book was Bill Fox. As a former Washington bureau chief for the *Toronto Star*, former Ottawa bureau chief for Southam Newspapers, and a former fellow of the Shornestein Media Center at Harvard and the Columbia School of Journalism, Bill's facility with the nuances of American and Canadian political discourse and the media could not have been more helpful.

My colleagues at Gluskin Sheff and Associates Inc., Toronto, the investment firm where I am an advisor, have been to a fault generous as to time and understanding. Ira Gluskin, Gerald Sheff, Alan Schwartz, and Harvey Bernstein have offered insights and perception that always enrich.

My old friend from our years spent serving Bob Stanfield, Bill Liaskas, has spent endless hours talking through many of the ideas in this book. Mark McQueen, my colleague from the Prime Minister's Office, and now an investment banker, has been equally generous with his time. He is probably less in agreement with much of this effort than with the core premises of the new right, although in the most humane and practical of ways. Rich Willis, an old friend, long-time small "c" conservative, and prominent party activist, is also well to the right of my position. Nevertheless, he has been characteristically liberal with the skills forged in him by his Jesuit graduate school professors in testing my hypotheses and arguments.

Shira Herzog of Toronto and Jim Hume of Calgary, both of the Kahanoff Foundation, have helped me better understand the potential role of community and of civic infrastructure and volunteer initiative relative to a truly balanced and sane society. While their interests and the foundation's are utterly non-partisan and completely philanthropic, my exposure through them to the issue of community clearly helped me see more clearly the pathways that link individual freedom to collective responsibility.

My view of American politics has been enhanced by two friends with immense reach and depth in the field. Bob Teeter, the founder of Market Opinion Research and long-time policy and strategic advisor to moderate Republicans from governors to senators and presidents, whose counsel is continuously sought by corporate and political America, has helped me come to some understanding of the shaping and fragmenting of mainstream Republicanism. His experience as a strategic advisor to moderate conservatives in Canada has given him a unique perspective on the strains of moderation and their challenges in both Canada and the U.S., from which I and others have benefited. Bob Odell, a veteran advisor and fundraiser for Republicans like Bush and Dole, has added the further perspective of the relationships between business and politics in America that could not have been more helpful.

That being said, I do not want to imply that anyone listed above necessarily agrees with the views I have expressed in this book or the ways I have chosen to express them. Omissions, mistakes, excesses, or imbalances are mine and mine alone.

Those whose influence I benefited from deserve no blame for any judgment, phrase, or approach I have chosen.

Any effort of this kind, even one as modest as this, requires encouragement and inspiration to reach fruition. In this category, I am seriously in some people's debt.

My editor at Stoddart, Don Bastian, was patient, elegant, and thoughtful in the gaps he had me fill and the matters of tone and substance he encouraged me to address. Jack Stoddart himself, someone I fear may not even be a conservative at all, added a measure of enthusiasm and passion to the project that was truly energizing. Perry Goldsmith, my literary agent, provided invaluable counsel on moving the project forward.

Vicki Ryce, my assistant in Kingston, devoted many hours to processing the manuscript, assisted at a crucial point by Angela Bearance. Shelley Pilon helped repeatedly on the research side of the ledger, as she did with my first book.

But through all of this, four people closest to me, and two other of God's creatures, sustained both the soul and the spirit: my older brother Brian, who as a magazine publisher is officially apolitical, but as a brother is always a great source of encouragement; my older, older brother Seymour, whose "painterly" (as he would describe it) views of what matters in life always refresh; my long-suffering partner and the love of my life, Donna, whose spirit, love, advice, and support are the candles that can light any night; and my daughter, Jacqueline, whose humor, questions, and sheer enthusiasm for life and people make her sarcasm about Dad's boring books ("Let me get this straight, Dad, another book about conservatism? Another page turner?") more than bearable.

And, in the early mornings and late nights when various drafts of various chapters get read and written and redrafted, two Bouviers, an elegant eight-year-old lady called Angel, and a bouncy and inelegant year-and-a-half pup called Charlotte, have been constant companions —Angel, usually sleeping through my reading out loud of various chapters, and Charlotte (alias Charlie) usually preferring to bounce or chew a very old tennis ball. For that disregard, and the healthy humility it helps ensure at most times — always pertinent to a traditional conservative — I am forever grateful.

KINGSTON
SEPTEMBER 1997

Introduction

When I traveled the country in the spring of 1996, I was astounded by two things. The first was that anyone had bought or read my recently published book, *No Surrender*; the second was that it made the bestseller lists. I was also struck by how many non-conservatives and conservatives alike said they wished I had written more of chapter 12, which dealt at some length with the differences between the neoconservatives and traditional Tories. Time and again in book stores, on university campuses, on talk radio, people would say, "We need more of chapter 12. We want to hear and read more about the real choices on the conservative spectrum."

Slowly, with the help of many well-wishers, letters from conservatives of all ages, and the critical notice (good and bad) received by the book, I felt the stirrings of courage to communicate a broader view of conservativism.

That feeble courage was enhanced by a profound discouragement bred during the 1996 presidential campaign in the United States by the way previously mainstream American Republicans had been made captive to divisive brands of conservatism, crushing decent candidates almost from the start. Good people, like Colin Powell, were ambushed before they could get their horses out of the stable.

In the United Kingdom, John Major's decent conservatism was being ambushed by Eurosceptic nationalists, dampening the kind of political progress that should have been fueled by Britain's significant economic gains under Conservative governments.

And in my own country, Canadian Progressive Conservative strength was being diluted by those who earnestly favored a regrouping of conservative forces along a narrow right path that wavered at the extremes of regionalism, anti-Quebec denial, and some xenophobia.

I began to see underlying patterns, broad lines that would help decipher the strategy of division and narrowness advanced by some on the new right.

For the purposes of this effort I divide the actual conservative spectrum of North America in the following way:

(1) Tories, Mainline Republicans (the Old Right). Small "c" conservatives who believe in the importance of a balance between freedom and responsibility. While for limited government, this group does not denigrate or dismiss the importance of government and other institutions like religion, the military, or the business sector in the larger cause of equality of opportunity and some measure of fairness. This group favors a broad pluralism in society, eschews liberal naiveté about big government, and in its interest in law and stability has no illusions about the need to control the worst aspects of human nature.

(2) Neoconservatives, Reformers, Nativists (the New Right).
Taking their inspiration from the excessive classical exaltation of the "individual" in nineteenth-century liberalism, this group values freedom as the core value — far more than responsibility to each other or to the common good. Their approach is to diminish the apparent efficacy of any expression of common interest that emerges through the use of democratically elected government. They prefer

policies and decisions that significantly favor individual freedom in all areas except when in conflict with their moral code. And in that regard, they view too much pluralism in terms of lifestyle and values as a threat to a moral code they are prepared to use the state and laws to impose. The enemies they try to create are usually foreign or subversive rather than systemic and local.

Surely it is high time we took stock of the onslaught of the new right and began to reflect on how its worst excesses might be contained.

The United States and Canada have both been battered by this serious form of extremism in the past half decade. We have faced excesses on the right similar to the anti-communist excesses in the '50s and just as corrosive. The new excess has trafficked in polarization — the creation of division for its own sake — and in that process has diminished the balance and civility of our democratic systems, eroding public faith in government overall.

This can be found in the way in which neoconservatives have opposed welfare rather than simply opposing welfare fraud, or in the way they expend no energy trying to bridge the gap between traditional private medicare that leaves millions uninsured and some modest measure of universal protection.

In Canada this is manifested by their inability to embrace accommodation with Quebec and, in some instances, to encourage separatism and centrifugal tensions elsewhere in the country. Throughout North America the new right embraces privatization without regard to specific costs and benefits on any case by case basis. It tends often to polarize on issues like fair taxation, immigration, public education, and religion in the schools.

The new right's intellectual core developed with the prominence, writing, and intellectual agitation of the neoconservatives in the late 1960s and early 1970s. It emerged from a core division in traditional American liberalism on issues like black nationalism, continuing Vietnam-focused campus disorder, and the view that many Great Society and War on Poverty programs had not been terribly successful.

George McGovern's takeover of the Democratic party in 1972 and his massive defeat both repelled Democrats from his form of liberalism and from the party that continued to embrace it. A black militancy grew in some Democratic circles, and many of the neoconservatives, like Irving Kristol, Nathan Glazer, or Norman Podhoretz, felt uncomfortable with the anti-Semitism that existed on the fringes of black militancy.

The extremism apparent in much of the new

left (tacit support for Black Panthers or Vietcong) produced liberals no longer comfortable sharing the liberal intellectual part of the spectrum with radicals. Hence the emergence of the new or neoliberals, whose ideas appeared on the pages of *Commentary* magazine. The new conservatives or neoconservatives focused on the need for a new realism at home — especially in social programs — and a less timid approach, post the debacle of Vietnam, to Soviet adventurism abroad.

There is certainly nothing dishonorable or illogical in these roots. It is what has grown since that is so clearly the threat to the cause of moderation, tolerance, democracy, and community.

Despite honorable roots, the process of polarization this engendered, and the specific instruments of polarity and extremism it helped, perhaps unwittingly, to create — like Buchananism, the Christian Coalition, or the more extreme elements of Reform in Canada — now do serious damage to a more reasoned and thoughtful debate.

The debilitating impact of this on the quality of our political choice in North America has also led to a broader intolerance of legitimate dissent, or of any pursuit of common ground or appeal to social cohesion. The arrogance of assuming that there can be only one way on economic or social policy has quickly spawned an intolerance of anyone with other views.

Some socialists and liberals have fought back to defend their political views on how we organize society. Sadly, both Democrats in the U.S. and Liberals and some New Democrats in Canada have embraced the path of least political resistance; in doing so they have narrowed and diminished the debate over competing approaches to government. President Clinton's abandonment of welfare in America to lure center-right voters to his coalition, Ontario Premier Bob Rae's decision to legislate retroactively an end to previously signed collective agreements, Prime Minister Jean Chretien's slashing of health transfers to the provinces — all these actions reflected an abandonment of traditional principles by titular liberal and socialist leaders. The collapse of some of the center-left does not aid the balance of the public policy debate.

◆

I write this conservative analysis of the danger of the neoconservative *putsch* because I believe that neoconservative excess has not only attacked the very traditions of a moderate, democratic, and tolerant conservatism but is also threatening the range and depth of democratic debate itself.

It is for mainstream Conservatives in Canada and Republicans in the United States to address this extreme distortion of cohesive conservative ideals in a way that does not destroy the good with the bad. The liberals and socialists would like nothing better than for traditional conservatism to be at war with its own extremes. After all, nothing would better ensure the perpetual re-election of Liberals in Canada or Democrats in the U.S. A destructive cycle on both sides of the border would then continuously feed on itself. Further fragmentation would surely follow the perpetual exile of Conservatives and Republicans from the different executive branches of government. The purveyors of religion-based politics could make common cause with their class-based allies on the far right to promote ideas that exalt divisions while negating those common values and virtues that play a uniting and motivating role in any civil society.

I am not thinking of Thatcher, Reagan, or Mulroney, who had little choice but to lean right to pull their governments back from their predecessors' political and fiscal regimes, which were either incompetent, spendthrift, or both.

I am thinking of today's purveyors of a selfish barbed-wire politics, one that seeks to destroy the conservative ideal that places order at the center of a universe where individual freedom and social responsibility coexist in real balance.

That balance is about compassion, hope, sharing,

and the true purposes of civilized life — it is about tolerance and equality of opportunity.

Eradicating that balance and replacing it with the law of the jungle is what neoconservatism has been and is all about. Economic growth without jobs is part of this new law. Industrial rationalization without income security for the victims is a corollary of this law. If institutionalized waste was the liberals' key fiscal weakness, then institutionalized greed may well be the neoconservatives' core weakness.

This essay is about taking back the battlefield of political debate from those who would carpet bomb with arrogance, insensitivity, and the language of division. It is about making the case for a civil conservatism that reflects rather than negates the very best of the human spirit, while suffering no naiveté about the worst.

Civil conservatism speaks to the human condition at its most humane, its most confident, its most outgoing and sensitive. It is not the foxhole neoconservative politics that fears and alienates all those with differing views or economic interests.

In the civil conservative world, individuals see themselves as part of a society in which community and responsibility coexist as means and ends with profit and freedom. This conservatism seeks for an order which that kind of coexistence can achieve. It seeks for the real benefits to productivity, stability, social justice, and opportunity which that order will bring. This conservatism is about a core defence of democracy — and the right within a democracy to have genuine differences of view. It is comfortable with open debate, not obsessed with restricting expression. It is about a democratic conservatism and a pluralist conservatism.

It is time to wrest the initiative from the purveyors of selfishness, division, and denial who call themselves neoconservatives. It is time to put ideas to work for people and set aside the proposition that people's opportunities must be constrained by the rigidity of narrow ideology.

Something else occurred to me that spring of 1996 as I traveled across Canada: that if mainstream conservatives fail to confront the new right with enthusiasm, no one else will — which would inevitably result in the dissolution of mainstream conservatism in most moderate and thinking people's minds and usher in a new period of center-left backlash and reaction.

This is why the debate must be joined.

1

In Defence of Democratic Debate

The anxiety Marxists had about the negative impact of religion as a dangerous opiate that might inspire people to a morality above and beyond the true dictatorship of the proletariat has had a remarkable parallel in the recent neoconservative anxiety about democratic choice.

That credo, as advanced by more extreme neoconservatives, suggests that deliberation in politics — the process in which elections, political parties, candidates, and manifestos represent instruments of choice; in which voters actually have freedom to choose, and choices to make — is no longer affordable. The credo argues that politics is no longer a debate about which *ends* we all want, but only about which *means* and what *instruments* we might choose to achieve the indisputable ends of lower deficit, less government, more profit, higher efficiency, and increased productivity. As if by focusing on what are essentially constructive ends one can obscure the need for a crucial debate on whether these actually *are* ends or means.

In the United States, some tax exempt and tax deductible foundations publish study after study that assess, criticize, or undermine much of public policy. For these groups of thinkers, if a program does not diminish government, lower taxes, reduce deficits, enhance profits and productivity, well, then, it is part of the problem and not part of the solution. This chant is pervasive and now deeply a part of our culture throughout North America. It was once suggested to me by Clare Westcott, a longtime aide to Premier Bill Davis of Ontario, that the Harvard Business School has done more to harm democracy than the Communist party. That is a little unfair to Harvard, but not to the rhetorical excess explicit in mass 1980s business school theory. Mass neoconservative absolutism is guilty of a similar excess.

The problem is not that productivity, profit increases, reduced taxes, less government, and reduced debt are bad things. They are, in fact, very good things. But at the very best, at the farthest possible reach of their value and benefit, these policy choices are not ends at all. They are not goals. They are not purposes. They are simply means to be used in public and private policy towards achieving the kind of society we are trying to build, reflective of the values we share.

Without that fundamental vision — without that precise and all-encompassing purpose — these means are merely road signs to nowhere, a route that leads to no place in particular, except to more of the same.

Surely when you let road signs and means occupy the political space that should be occupied by purposes and goals, you have obliterated the need for any real democracy. It has been my own experience in politics, business, and academe that the continuing search for the right vision, combined with the ongoing debate over which ideas will serve the public interest, is what fuels creativity, democracy, and progress. End the search, and you begin to lose sight of democracy itself.

Democracy is, when expressed in politics, a civil argument about the future. Not just about how to get there, but about where "there" truly is. And, more importantly, about which version of "there" is the right version.

A society that is civil, restrained, humane, orderly, and compassionate may well imply efforts to diminish the gap between rich and poor as well as generating wealth and growth. A society that values choice and responsibility may be more open to community responses to problems, as well as the importance of individual freedom as a central and overarching social value.

These are debates Americans and Canadians have the right to have — at election and other times; setting these aside in favor of a sterile argument solely about which means to use, and at what pace, is a limiting of democracy itself. This cop-out aids those with a narrow agenda on both the far right and far left who want an erosion of politics and democracy and a simple objective. For those on the far right, it's sustained return on capital; for those on the far left, it's a pure class warfare, untroubled by other competing more moderate agendas around social justice or local autonomy. The relative blending in the U.S. of Democrats and Republicans on goals, with only an incidental disagreement on means, mirrors the similarity in Canada between the Liberals, New Democrats, and Conservatives when in government, all essentially buying into the same goals, again with only minor variation on the means.

No wonder voter participation in the United States continues to fall and voter cynicism in Canada to rise. A politics that offers only choices over means and no debate on the ends is no politics at all. Without a politics of meaning, some will question the very purposes of democracy and civil society. If the real choices are made at meetings of corporate boards or union locals — no doubt in the honest but narrow discharge of their fiduciary responsibilities to their shareholders or members — who will speak for the rest of us who may not fall into these constituencies? If on the issue of purpose, other political parties, leaders, and locally elected representatives are to be rendered irrelevant, why have democracy at all? As some businessmen from Asia pointed out at a CEOs seminar in Barcelona in 1996, Western-style democracy is hopelessly inefficient, costly, often not terribly meritocratic, and often fails to bring forward the best or most competent leadership. If the choices to be made center merely on the best means to achieve fiscal ends determined elsewhere, then surely policy can best be decided by experts. And surely those experts can simply be retained by those making the real decisions outside the democratic process.

This efficiency *über alles* paradigm would seem quite logical, efficient, less costly, and more productive. And think of it: we would be rid of all those politicians constantly parading about, more ego than substance, more focused on ritual gamesmanship than what really matters to you and me as taxpayers and voters. None among us should be surprised that this view would or could gain popularity. The inescapable result of one-idea politics is no politics at all.

If the economic purposes of civil society are established only by international money markets and the social purposes defined by the religious right in both Canada and the United States, there would in fact be little need for sustained, broadly embraced, and meaningful political debate. Inexorable universal laws would render politics obsolete. And those on the extreme left and right would celebrate as their ultimate victory the death of politics. There would be no need for dissent, compromise, common ground, tolerance, or for putting water in one's wine.

Such a politics, or non-politics, sustains the self-righteous nature of narrowly held extreme views. Republicans in the United States and Conservatives in Canada are, especially when in opposition, attracted by the clarity and simplicity of one-dimensional, simple answers to complex problems. They mouth the ritual incantations of lower debt, no deficit, less government, higher profits, greater productivity as if mere repetition will bring happiness and deliverance for all people. This is not conservatism.

Conservatism is about the organic nature of society — the linkage between family, freedom, tolerance, civility, economic pursuit, law, order, tradition, and opportunity. It is about seeing any society as a living, breathing body with different needs, opportunities, and relationships. It embraces values about human nature and the need for structures that restrain the worst and liberate the best in people across the social spectrum. It embraces the core view that duty, responsibility, and order are the non-negotiable foundations upon which genuine freedom and opportunity are built.

Mainstream and moderate conservatives on both sides of the 49th parallel have not in the past been afraid to embrace the larger questions of how and why a society exists and for what purposes institutions should exist. Socialists and Conservatives truly differ on the answers to these questions, but every generation of them must ask and try to master them.

◆

It was the establishment Liberals and Democrats who have classically focused on means as ends in and of themselves, based on their profoundly naive belief in the perfectibility of the human condition — and in the benign decency of unhindered human nature. Ironically, it is in this very naiveté that the roots of the neoconservative attack on true political choice can be found.

And now, neoconservatives at the extremes of politics in the U.S. and Canada have co-opted classical liberal fascination with the "how" and imposed a new absolutism that oppresses any debate on the "why."

This process was expressed in the rapid neoconservative and extreme fundamentalist ambush of the Colin Powell presidential candidacy, and in Canada in the effort to radicalize Canadian conservatism by a focused neoconservative strike force seeking to dilute and then absorb the mainstream Progressive Conservatives.

How did this change take place? What exactly are the roots of this new neoconservative absolutism?

What American liberals differed on after World War II focused initially on whether Russia could be dealt with benignly or only as a foe. That difference produced great debates about the true nature of communism and the core goals of American democracy.

As the paranoia and anxiety were exacerbated by the Cold War — and not always without some justification — American liberalism was divided as it faced McCarthy's malignant search for communists under the bed. The advance of the communists in Korea, KGB intrigue throughout the world, Soviet oppression in the Eastern European theater, the huge strength in their region of the Chinese — all these conspired to feed an intense conflagration among liberals in the United States about the choices to be made.

Was the intimidation handed out by the McCarthy hearings an appropriate response to the global communist threat, including the stealing of atomic secrets? Or, as some liberals believed, was it an excessive and offensive tyranny imposed on those only guilty — if at all — of merely holding a dissident political view? The debate around blacklisting was also a defining moment of American liberalism, emanating in great lines of argument over foreign policy and its implications for U.S. democracy.

That debate deepened around the Eisenhower anxiety relative to the military industrial complex, Kennedy and the Vietnam war, and consistent failures in U.S. policy around Cuba. But, ever so subtly, the debate, which had been mitigated as between liberals through their collective unity on the issues of segregation and civil rights, slowly began to be eclipsed by a debate between traditional conservatives and liberals relative to the best approach to domestic issues like race, poverty, social spending, and urbanization.

Perhaps the first true crossover was that of

J. Patrick Moynihan, who in the White House, as both a Kennedy moderate and domestic advisor in the Nixon administration, began a large part of the intellectual tradition that became the honorable roots of early neoliberal and neoconservative debate. In its early days, this tradition was about new ideas: new frames of reference and a refreshing frankness in matters of public and social policy.

But from this point of departure came the twists and turns of personal ambition, intellectual entrepreneurialism, hucksterism, young writers on the make, and the rarefied hothouse atmosphere of New York intellectuals, all of which began to spawn a new kind of abrasive, corrosive guerrilla conservatism that often valued colorful rhetoric over intellectual rigor — and certainly valued the intensity of views held over the objectivity of the analyses behind those views.

The excesses of the Kennedy and Johnson regimes, the amiable incompetence of the Carter administration, the association of Democrats with the disasters that were Vietnam and the Bay of Pigs afforded mainstream Republicanism of the Nixon and Bush variety, and even the more conservative but essentially people-friendly and upbeat Republicanism of Ronald Reagan, a sustained period of political dominance in the White House. Yet, persistent deficits, intensified battles over abortion, and the emergence of the religious right turned mainstream Republicans into the real targets, as neoconservatives began their struggle for a political dominance unimpeded by the moderation of cohesive coalition politics.

All of which was a sustainable part of the pluralism of American democracy until the disappearance of the Soviet Union as prime focus of external threat to the United States. The Soviet decline was the result of a genuine conservative success in the NATO anchors of the U.K., U.S., and Canada in arraying a resolve on defence spending and planning that could no longer be met strategically by a Soviet Union in pursuit of even minimal consumer gains for its own people. That victory, activated during the Gorbachev years, liberated the neoconservative forces to address domestic policy in the United States. They could have focused on the ongoing challenges of the race issue, growing levels of poverty and illiteracy. Instead, and not surprisingly, their muscular rhetoric, previously aimed at Soviet adventurism and third world fellow travelers, was trained on the new enemy — American moderation.

All the evils of contemporary American reality — crime, debt, social program waste, or dysfunction — became the fault of moderates among both Democrats and Republicans. The attack on moderation became synonymous with neoconservative rhetoric.

And so, as if for lack of an external enemy, neoconservatives turned their rhetoric on the moderate policies of coalition politics. This was aided and encouraged by middle class and boomer angst, by media fragmentation that produced purely political and evangelical specialty channels, and by the scourge of the Political Action Committees and right-wing foundations that engaged in tax deductible advocacy activities well beyond the meaning of philanthropy.

The increasingly well-financed neoconservative juggernaut moved ever steadily ahead.

In Canada, the election of establishment Liberals in the late '60s, at the federal level, usually propped up by excessive majorities in Quebec and tied to massive government interaction, bred an anti-Quebec, anti-Central Canada faction that plagued both Liberals and Progressive Conservatives. Ongoing constitutional challenges and negotiation over an almost twenty-year period inflated western Canadian alienation and created fecund growth conditions for the neoconservative virus. Profligate Liberal spending in the '60s, '70s, and '80s prompted debt levels that saw even meaningful spending reductions in the '80s and '90s overshadowed by rampant growth in interest on the debt. The wrongful association of profligacy with social programs combined with wide regional economic variations to fuel a western-based fragmentation of conservatives. In the west, new, shrill voices harkened back in part to the populist, somewhat simplistic post-Depression Social Credit parties. The mainstream, more Tory, Conservative party lost strength to extremists at the fringes who despite the moderation of most in the Reform party could not disengage from their early, more extreme, roots.

In both Canada and the United States in more recent times the subsequent fragmentation was contributed to by the sheer size of Republican and Conservative victories, the wide swath of support that came the way of mainstream Reagan and Mulroney majorities.

Reagan's coalition so broadened Republicans beyond their 20-21% core vote that by the time they were in the mid-40% range in terms of base vote, their coalition had more than its fair share of nut bars, religious extremists, and hard right ideologues. In the Canadian Tory case, the breadth of the Mulroney coalition, so far beyond usual Tory limits, could not possibly be held together by a leader less willful and less competent than he — as his successor, Kim Campbell, clearly was.

◆

The roots, then, of present excess lie in a confluence of events that neoconservatives have masterfully taken advantage of since the mid-1980s. Broad conservative majorities on both sides of the border allowed greater market segmentation. The evaporation of the Soviet Union as a common enemy allowed neoconservatives to brandish their rhetorical excesses against moderates on their own side of the spectrum. Excesses by Liberal and Democratic governments encouraged more radical responses. Honorable neoliberal and neoconservative roots were hacked at by a new and more virulent form of neoconservative excess that could only win through polarization and the encouragement of division.

Mainstream conservatives reacted too slowly, or with insufficient competence, to hold the center. Though not related to each other, Preston Manning's Reform party in Canada and Ross Perot's Reform party in the United States embraced populist determinism to hobble Kim Campbell's Conservatives and George Bush's Republicans. Between 15 and 20% of the vote was sliced off the conservative mainstream in the elections of 1992 in the U.S. and 1993 in Canada, with the result that Liberals and Democrats replaced conservatives in both federal elections. This established one unalterable rule in the politics of North America. When excessive right-wing populism surges, liberals win elections.

2

The Tyranny of the Simple Idea

When the enemy was communism and its dehumanizing oppression of societies and people — particularly in its totalitarian Soviet application — simply being opposed made good sense. But is the demise of Soviet imperialism a rationale for adapting a simplistic opposition to all activities of the state, or the community, or to the broader social responsibility we share?

Some neoconservatives seem to believe that the answer is at least a partial yes. And the intensity of their belief fuels an attack on moderation itself, and even on a limited role for the state.

Set aside the purposely comic antics of the Rush Limbaugh school of media contrivance, in which getting attention through ridicule is infinitely more important than content quality. Look instead at the Republican party's Contract with America after the midterm congressional elections in 1994. Simplicity was the appeal and division the modus operandi in this program, which promised simplistic solutions to violent crime, bureaucratic waste and regulation, and other problems in a way that unnecessarily polarized Americans.

That contract focused not on an inclusive view of society — which would have been the traditional conservative approach — but on a divisive view that clearly sought to build Republican electoral momentum by subtly exploiting economic, class, and racial divisions. Unlike Eisenhower, or the early Nixon, or George Bush in 1988, there was no Republican appeal to healing or pulling the nation together. It was, instead, a polarizing appeal, aimed at fanning interclass anxiety and harvesting the votes of both the well-to-do and the highly anxious and ethnocentric. As such it was a departure from tradition Republican politics, much more in the Southern Democrat George Wallace tradition. It would have made Teddy Roosevelt deeply uncomfortable. But it was the logical extension of the easy and muscular politics of the new right since the days of Irving Kristol and Norman Podhoretz: a departure from the more civil and less facile approach of earlier proponents of the old right like William F. Buckley, Jr.

Easy answers to complex problems ruled the day.

The new right had easy answers to all problems. If Jews and blacks were experiencing tensions, it was simply because blacks were becoming anti-Semitic. If poverty was increasing among some groups, it was simply more their fault than ever before (the poor lack moral fiber to want to work). If there was corruption or waste in federal or state activities, it was all because regulation and public policy were bad per se. If the public school system was in decline, it was because integrated public schools were a bad thing, as was public non-confessional education. Too many abortions were solely the result of pro-choice laws where they exist, and public tolerance of promiscuity. Despite the huge economic pressures, traditional single breadwinner "wife stay at home" family structures were painted as the best solution. Despite what most Americans saw as the legitimate right of women to equality in the workplace, the new religious right artfully tied women who worked to family breakdown and the excessive costs of child care. And in the search for simpler solutions, in the post-Watergate, post-Carter period, when government at the center was seen as either corrupt or incompetent, a religious right neoconservative lobby increased in its velocity, intensity, and clout.

Ronald Reagan began his career as a Democrat, a broadcaster, and a union leader. The populist, well-communicated idealism of his early days survived his re-creation as a California Republican. His pleasant, decent, and likely genuine disposition was an unwitting cover for the darker side of neoconservative excess that took root in many parts of America's core political culture. Conservative think tanks like the American Enterprise Institute that were thoughtful and substantive, and quite uninterested in the politics of intolerance or greed, were quickly overtaken by groups like the Christian Coalition, whose ideological agenda was driven by both self-interest and loose American tax laws. The wealthy had, if they needed it, a new way to gain influence in American public policy: they could pay others to offer simple solutions to complex problems; they could support political candidates, by funding Political Action Committees. Right-wing "think tanks" were set up from which congressional aides, White House advisors, and even members of the cabinet could be appointed or to which they might go. Some conservatives would argue that this only replicated the influence established by the center and center-left like the Brookings Institute or the Kennedy School of Government.

The hundreds of millions being spent (with IRS

subsidy via deductibility) to sustain this neoconservative viewpoint was unprecedented in U.S. history.

Self-interest here is apparent. Those who benefit from incompetent or impotent government and government regulation stand to gain the most from wave upon wave of new, seemingly intellectual arguments arrayed, at whatever cost, against any role for the state along with any innovation or refinement of that role. Dollars spent in support of this anti-all-government cause produce huge paybacks, hundreds of times more than the cost of the think tanks themselves. Whether it is the producer of firearms, or those who want less regulation in financial markets, or the many companies or foreign interests that wish for unlimited access to the U.S. consumer, government with its legitimacy always under attack is the government they most benefit from.

◆

And the cycle continues. As long as there is no pluralist conservative appeal for a more civil and informed debate, the forces of moderation or innovation — be they of the Jack Kemp, or the Colin Powell, variety — may well avoid or be discouraged from any direct engagement. And, more ominously, the possibility of a true outbreak on the isolationist, xenophobic, and bigoted extreme that many associate with Pat Buchanan is enhanced as the level of low-grade animosity towards community and government is stoked and enhanced.

It is not a long march from opposing school busing to blaming all problems on immigration, illegal or otherwise. It is not a long reach from protectionism and opposition to all forms of international or collective sovereignty like the United Nations or World Trade Organization and the isolationist and nativist stand of Mr. Buchanan. We are only engaged here in a way station along the same narrow road that always leads to the same dead end.

Conservatives who were troubled about the Buchanan message in the last set of presidential primaries have good reason to be deeply troubled. He reached out to a xenophobic, bigoted, nativist United States that had as little time for immigrants or trading relationships abroad as it did for central bankers with Wall Street pedigrees or non-Anglo Saxon names. And he missed no chance to give the pots a stir.

Some neoconservatives who were troubled really had only themselves to blame. Buchanan and his view of America's interests did not hatch overnight. Buchanan himself emerged from a simple "right is always right" mindset in the '80s that replaced reason with nostrums and solid analysis with raw ideological piffle. That is the stuff of anti-immigration crusades, two guns in every home, and to hell with slant-eyed foreigners. And that is the source of Buchanan's momentum — along with anxieties in the northeast about jobs evaporating while profits soared. The disconnect between economic growth and individual middle class opportunity and security — itself a gap justified and exalted by neoconservatives — became the rich soil in which Buchananism could grow.

So the industry of simple answers like the principle of the invisible hand of the marketplace operates on its own self-justifying rhythm. Its main goals are to prevent new public policy and, where possible, destroy the credibility of old public policy. The targets of this industry are broad, including academics, welfare recipients, civil servants, policy wonks, teachers, public sector workers and, on occasion, large corporations, foreigners, and trade unions. Their foot soldiers of decency, who are rarely criticized and often lionized, are the fundamentalist clergy, the family, the farmer, the entrepreneur, and the police.

◆

Contrast this with traditional U.S. conservatism that was not against institutions that served broad public purposes. While traditional conservatives did oppose the separation of church and state, they came to value both religious observance and, over time, religious tolerance.

Traditional conservatism did not view all those in the public sector as evil or a drain on society. Its positive belief in the importance of the police did not extend to a cavalier disregard for the issue of civil liberties or the rights of those who lawfully dissent.

In other words, traditional conservatives would worry about the excesses of bureaucracy without being against *all* government. We could be against excesses in welfare, for instance, without opposing welfare completely.

But that is the kind of moderation neocons have squeezed out of the debate — and the kind of moderation without which U.S. conservative politics is made more narrow.

In Canada the polarization process also proceeds apace. The traditional focus on the duality of Canada's English- and French-speaking roots has been replaced by the far right with a difference-smothering equality doctrine that opposes the basis of the core compromise that is Canada. So Prince Edward Island, with 120,000 residents, and Quebec, with almost eight million mostly francophone residents, should have precisely the same legislative authority. This is based on the equality of all provinces and citizens. Of course what is ignored is this: when the smallest province has the same clout as the most populous, the voters in the larger province lose their democratic equality to the voters in smaller provinces.

The far right in Canada has focused on tougher punishment for young offenders, the allegedly central role illegal immigration plays in geometrically increasing Canada's problems, and an utterly isolationist view of Canada's defence and international obligations. They have championed an insensitive view of Quebec's aspirations within Canada, and those of aboriginal Canadians, and have broken from the traditional and until now successful tradition of accommodation and compromise. They are profoundly pro-American — which is in itself not a bad thing — but insensitive to the many excesses that America's approach on issues like gun control or health care produce for America's most vulnerable. They are sustained often by some individuals who are themselves the American-financed intellectual spear-carriers for the neocon movement.

Canada's Reform movement — the neocon front — has become a purveyor of a populist view; the political party, quite devoid of any governing policies, serves as a vehicle for the hot button views of the day. This arrangement has the added virtue of condoning any excess that erupts in vox populi. Gays, people who are visible minorities, ethnics, immigrants — all susceptible to the harsh and often bigoted wisdom of the open line radio talk show — find themselves on occasion in the sights of individual Reformers. While the official rebuke of those who go over the line has been swift and thorough, the need to do so is regular enough so as to assure those of more extreme views that one need not worry about who the Reform party *really* is. While the party is still limited to a regional base, the clarity of its populism — plus the inherent momentum that the politics of protest can provide — maintains their potential at meaningful levels. The risk to Canada is far more serious than a realignment along the left-right continuum; it could well be the breakup of the country itself.

Quebec separatists, who have been active in North American politics since the eighteenth century, have always been frustrated by the lack of interest in the separatist option shown by two groups. One group is the majority of moderate Quebec nationalists who wish only to preserve Quebec's majority French language, culture, civil code, and civilization, without necessarily becoming a separate country. The other has been a moderate cross section of Canadians outside Quebec who see no contradiction between the contemporary expression of Canadian federalism and the legitimate regional and cultural aspirations of Quebecers and other Canadians in other provinces. These moderate groups still seek accommodation. But they are being assaulted by the simplistic polarizations of the far right's new intolerant populism.

The long and successful history of Canada, dubbed repeatedly by the United Nations the country with the highest quality of life in the world, is a series of compromises that go right back to the British response to the fall of Quebec in 1759. The British success against France's garrison in Quebec, more the product of France's failure to resupply, produced the Quebec Act of 1774 that protected the French language, the Roman Catholic Church, and the education system of Quebec. That, in large measure, kept French Quebec from having any interest in supporting the subsequent American Revolution and began a process of compromises and codeterminations between the European founding peoples who joined with Canadian aboriginals to repel Americans in the War of 1812 and build a country. The spirit of moderation on the French-English divide has inspired conservative, liberal, and socialist political traditions in Canada. It survived the pressures of conscription crisis during the wars, the rigidity of Pierre Trudeau's Cartesian and anti-nationalist regime, and many local disputes over minority rights.

But now the simplistic assault on those who deny that Quebec, as a Canadian province with the only majority French-speaking jurisdiction in all of North America, needs specific capacities to protect that language, culture, and civilization truly threatens the historic and successful record of compromise. The simple notion that all provinces are equal could truly cost Canada its national survival.

For North America the pursuit of simple answers to the complex issues of self-government, social justice, economic growth, and fiscal responsibility is both unbecoming and unproductive. It diminishes what we can do for ourselves and with each other. It diminishes any sense of common values or common achievement. All the successes of public policy, from public health care in Canada to social security in the United States, are simply attacked as horrible failures. Collective achievements count for nothing. Freedoms hard won from economic calamity are portrayed as excessive and unaffordable. The balancing forces of a civilized society are shunted aside. If it is not of the market, by the market, or for the market, it simply doesn't count.

This simplistic obsession is destroying both the

caliber of debate and the reach of our politics. Moderates like Arlen Spector or Christie Whitman face exorcism or ambush simply because they dare to be innovative or moderate.

Hope is replaced with harsh despairs. Optimism is replaced with cynical appeals to our worst fears.

The marketers of polarity are in full force.

If this were coming from the left, we would call it totalitarian.

3

Destroying the Postwar Consensus

The huge human, financial, and technical effort pitted against the Nazis did more than repel world tyranny and initiate a period of postwar expansion and reconstruction — as if all that were not enough. The success of the allies posed a new question to a world that had just emerged from the shadow of Nazi menace to the optimism of a new beginning. Surely if the massing of resources could defeat Hitler — a task that at times must have seemed close to hopeless — was it not self-evident that we could assemble resources and people to confront illness, illiteracy, homelessness, unemployment, and the financial stress of growing old?

The answer, which came from social and Christian

Democrats in Europe, from Gaullists and socialists in France, Progressive Conservatives and Liberals and Socialists in Canada, Tories and Labour in the U.K., and Democrats and Republicans in the U.S., was a resounding yes. There were, of course, differences as to nuance and tone and degree. But, whether from Mr. Truman or General Eisenhower, from Ontario's Premier Drew or Canada's Louis St. Laurent, whether from Bevan, Churchill, Macmillan, or Gaitskill, the gaps were about the rate of progress, or the specific application, not the task itself!

In a compelling and fascinating speech on October 5, 1946, to the Conservative party conference in Blackpool, Winston Churchill, then in opposition, put it this way:

"In fact, we seek so far as possible to make the status of the wage earner that of a partner rather than that of an irresponsible employee. It is in the interest of the wage earner to have many other alternatives open to him . . .

"Freedom of enterprise and freedom of service are not possible without elaborate systems of safeguards against failure, accident or misfortune. We do not seek to pull down imprudently the structures of society, but to erect balustrades upon the stairway of life, which will prevent helpless or foolish people from falling into the abyss . . .

"It is 38 years ago since I introduced the first Unemployment Insurance Scheme, and 22 years ago since, as Conservative Chancellor of the Exchequer, I shaped and carried the Widow's Pensions and reduction of the Old Age Pension from 70 to 65. We are now moving forward into another vast scheme of national [health] insurance, which arose, even in the stress of war from a Parliament with a great Conservative majority . . .

"We declare ourselves the unsleeping opponents of all class, all official or all party privilege . . ."*

(Clearly Mrs. Thatcher would have dismissed Sir Winston Churchill as a hopeless wet; Buchanan would likely have called him a Communist.)

It is part and parcel of neoconservative and neoliberal extremism and dishonesty in the '90s to diminish this reconstructive postwar consensus that broadly crossed party lines in the democracies and reflected a collective and individual will to build societies capable of far more than the Depression that in part led to World War II. Neoconservatives choose to simply call it all liberal spendthrift excess.

Moreover, after the war, resource- and infrastructure-rich North American economies experienced a boom in demand, profits, and tax yields that

---

*Churchill, Randolph, editor, *The Sinews of Peace*. Cassel and Company, London 1948.

meant they were awash in revenue at precisely the time the postwar social and economic requirement provided meaningful places for public policy to commit cash.

This was not, as some revisionists now argue, a case of the political class cynically seducing people with their own money. This was evidence of a public mood in which everyone in the veterans' generation had a right to full employment, to decent pensions, to good roads and homes — and their children had the right to good schools, health care, and broad opportunities.

Any political party or politician in the Western world who was insensitive to this was disconnected from the reality of public will and expectation. Today, the anti-government defeatism of the neo-conservative theologue conveniently argues that if public spending solved problems, then deficits and the size they have reached should mean we should have eradicated all social problems. This narrow argument implies that all problems exist within a sealed universe in place and time, and that once a problem is dealt with in one generation, it should not recur in the next.

This simple analysis fails to ask the more important question. Where would we be today if we had accepted widespread poverty, if we had failed to build schools and hospitals, if we had failed to ensure publicly in Canada against widespread catastrophic health costs, if the United States had not spent lavishly on its G.I. bills or social security? Would a world in the '70s or '80s, made up of indigent seniors, financially embarrassed veterans, young people with no place to go to school, and health care only for the more prosperous have been a better place for investment and growth? Would it have been as steady and superior a competitor, in the people's minds, with the excesses of totalitarian communism?

The very silly idea that work done on one generation's problems should mean no challenge to be faced in the next speaks to neoconservatism's absolutist preference for neat worlds and zero sum solutions. Denying the fact that as benefits carry on from generation to generation, so do costs, speaks simply to neoconservative intellectual dishonesty. Deficit funding for capital projects like schools, hospitals, hydroelectric dams, or highways will have costs that carry into the future as do the revenue- and benefit-producing assets of a productive and healthy society.

What a riveting grasp of human development the neoconservative movement fosters and advances! To extend this rule — and I once heard a distinguished Canadian business leader agree with this proposition — the money spent in children's hospitals on new and helpful procedures is quite inefficient, because when the patient is 50 or 60, something else will probably go wrong. So what's it all worth?

Other similar profundities in this neoconservative list might include such statements as: Spending public funds on snow removal is a misuse of taxpayers' money. The snow will come back. Or, while many of the parents of neoconservatives had the benefit of student loans or veterans' education bursaries, we should discontinue the programs because, well, it's an unfair subsidy to their grandchildren, and who benefits from this anyway? Or, spending public funds to help those without resources is of no real help because the poor are always with us.

This neocon, circular logic is of course missing in action when public funds are used to ensure company exports or bank deposits. Traditional conservatives applaud both these supports, because they promote stability and confidence. We are also not troubled when this same support is extended to the most vulnerable and disadvantaged among us.

This is not so much the politics of the old welfare state — which is a relic we should not want and cannot afford — but the politics of genuine social stability, surely the ultimate prerequisite for economic confidence, personal freedom and opportunity, investment, and productive industrial and technological innovation. If the absence of fair wages, social stability, and minimum standard of living were precursors of economic success, then Haiti would be a likely candidate for economic center of the hemisphere. (We should perhaps not be too hasty here. Impotent democracy, grinding poverty, and pistol-powered gangs may be closer to what some neoconservatives at the extremes truly prefer.)

◆

The counterargument to all this, in more rational terms, is the simple and quite respectable doctrine of sound and limited government. In the face of over-grasping, fiscally undisciplined, and overbearing governments, it is a theory, when judicially applied, that has much merit. And the use of this approach in moderation to force government to make choices does not imply that real policy choices are beyond the scope of democratic government. It is not immediately clear why for the neoconservatives such choices must always exclude investing in leveraging people out of poverty or investing in genuine equality of opportunity so as to always make room only for subsidy to industry or collapsing tax levels. What precisely is the inherent legitimacy of those who argue for this path? Why is their societal priority always beyond debate?

And, more importantly, where is the evidence that billions spent on social programs and infrastructure have been wasted while the billions spent on tax deferrals for corporate capital investment have been a stunning success? As a Tory, I applaud the use of deferred taxes to encourage capital spending, technological advance, and investment. Such a policy is not, however, always as useful in terms of outcome as intended, but that is no reason to stop all of it. The same rule applies to social spending.

Was the help given to millions of Americans and Canadians to move them from poverty to relative middle class comfort via student loans, better schools, subsidized universities a waste of time and money?

And what about seniors today? They live in relative comfort (at least until the neocons hack away at their net) as a direct result of decisions in the '60s about restructuring old age income. Was this a huge social policy mistake, or a clear victory of policy makers and societies that looked at old age indigence and decided it should be tolerated no more? If expenditures on infrastructure like clean water, organized public plumbing, and rural electrification were so wasteful, why are Canadians and Americans living longer, in greater health? Is that, too, a waste of precious dollars better spent on lower taxes for bond traders?

The younger neoconservative is unimpressed by these apparent social benefits; they are convinced there will be no similar benefits available to them — hence programs must be cut. And, the reasoning continues, if there are no programs of this nature in their future, then, quite frankly, they need higher incomes and less taxes if they are going to be able to provide for themselves.

It is a masterful circular argument.

First, attack the right and competence of government to contribute to equality of opportunity through programs like health care, education, or income security. Use the religious right to launch moral / family freedom / personal choice missiles against the government's role. Then argue that capital mobility, new technologies, and competitive pressures make whatever a society might try to do through its government intrinsically unaffordable, because the tax yields necessary can't be sustained, and lower cost industrial bases will lure jobs away.

And then, fully convince large segments of the population and some governments that they must no longer strive to help achieve any measure of equality of opportunity. Now you can further push citizens to want radically lower taxes and higher tax-free incomes as they can obviously count on *no* protection whatever from the worst excesses of a society whose social supports are in free fall.

The salience of this approach is of course sustained by the general belief, which appears to have accompanied the advent of taxes, that one is always overtaxed. It is an argument that plays to a sense of victimization most people easily feel. And to give credit where credit is due, the neoconservative movement in the United States and the Reform party in Canada have done excellent jobs dominating the marketplace of ideas on this issue — with response only from the center-left who, of course, with *their* excesses in support of equality of outcomes vs. equality of opportunity actually help make the neoconservative case.

◆

The traditional conservative response to this defeatist consensus is more relevant and appropriate.

It is, and it is consistent from Benjamin Disraeli to Churchill to Jack Kemp, from Nelson Rockefeller to Bill Davis, from George Bush to Peter Lougheed, from John Major to Brian Mulroney, that society is an organic whole, with its aggregate strengths and weaknesses linked to the strongest and weakest within society; that to view society in terms of "high potential" classes or persons of potential vs. those beyond hope is to disengage from the full meaning of society itself. The conservative view does not limit freedom to affirm social responsibility, seeing that it is no threat to freedom to attack the unfairness of a permanent underclass. In fact, the humanity that is expressed on behalf of society as a whole is its best bulwark against the instability of an entrenched and hopeless underclass, who have little to gain from an orderly and civil society. An orderly and civil society, where the vast majority have either achievement, economic opportunity, or both to sustain and motivate provides the most dependable platform for excellence, productivity, investment, and growth. Social justice cannot be a sometime product of free enterprise's upcycle. Its role is as the fundamental linkage between the forces of capitalist initiative and the benefits to all of social stability and individual opportunity.

Traditional conservatives promote this balance because they feel comfortable with none other. This balance does not give licence to wasteful administrations or overly centralized bureaucracies, but it surely does not countenance abdication from the duty to promote social justice.

Those who countenance or propose denying that duty have embraced a nihilistic ideology of social pessimism that dismisses neighborhoods, communities, political parties, and governments. All governments are flawed, in their view, and are therefore disposable. All have on occasion been populated by incompetent, self-seeking, and sometimes even evil people. It follows, neocons argue, that those flaws are systemic, universal, woven into the very fabric of these expressions of community themselves.

This principle dismissive of all government effort is worthy of careful and thoughtful review.

Let's apply it elsewhere.

Because some neoconservative think tanks are little more than fronts for industries and companies that stand to gain directly from government dysfunction, are all think tanks therefore hopelessly self-interested?

Because some evangelical clergymen have been found to be less than Christlike in their forthrightness on money, or somewhat disengaged from the Ten Commandments in their pursuit of the fairer sex, does that mean that the entire evangelical movement is corrupt?

Because some in the new American and Canadian right have been racist, bigoted, or homophobic — even totalitarian in their will to use the state (imagine!) to advance their narrow views on others — does that mean that the entire neoconservative movement can be dismissed as anti-human rights, or against equality before the law?

To all three questions, the answer is a resounding "No!" So, on what basis do neoconservatives on both sides of the world's longest undefended border dismiss government, community, public policy, and social responsibility as unsustainable? Or community as unworkable?

At best, it is the callowness of youth, the impatience of new wealth, or the enthusiasm of amateurs that sweeps so broadly.

At worst, it is the intolerance and excess of extremism.

As Tories prefer good manners in all things, I will hope it is the former.

The consensus that dominated the postwar period is less pervasive because the fiscal reality of the '70s — oil price shocks, inflationary pressures, interest rate pressures, and demographic realities — has made the consensus more challenging to sustain.

That reality may well suggest new approaches and instruments to achieve policy goals around social justice.

That reality is not, however, an argument for deserting the values upon which those hopes and aspirations are based.

Those values are fundamental to a society of opportunity, freedom, and economic growth. To desert them because defending them is more difficult would be to embrace a lesser view of what the partnership between enterprise and community can produce.

That lesser view, that diminished optimism, that early surrender in the face of difficulty tells us several things about many in the neoconservative mainstream.

They have discarded the role of the community and government in the pursuit of social justice because the politics of appealing to the culture of failure is easier and more politically rewarding.

They have used the simple idea of freedom as an escape hatch from the more difficult task of building a society where all have equality of opportunity. It is the kind of escape that has some of its roots in the isolationism that opposed America's entry into World War II.

They would rather run than fight.

They prefer surrender to engagement.

And, finally, it's a damn good thing they were not in charge during World War II.

4

Beyond the Economic Model

Postwar economic and social policy in North America has been about upward social mobility. Postwar immigration patterns to North America from all parts of the world have reflected the genuine and justified belief that the opportunity for economic opportunity and freedom in a stable society was incalculably better there than in places like the Ukraine, Italy, India, Pakistan, Germany, Indochina, or Central America. The underlying and core truth of that belief has been sustained by more than pure economics. It has been sustained by a host of social and political norms that helped make the growing economies possible and which, in turn, themselves benefited from the economic growth.

The development of American social infrastructure, such as schools, roads, and local government, also reflected the importance from the days of the American Revolution and beyond of local, community, and voluntary associations. De Tocqueville, the French analyst of post-Revolutionary America, noted it when he spoke of the voluntary associations and organizations that distinguished America from Europe in the eighteenth century. The importance of religious faith, local association, and unfettered enterprise conspired in America to produce an uncommon opportunity for individual immigrants and their families to build more rewarding and stable lives.

Compared with Europe, the United States was resource and geography rich. More importantly for many who came to America's shores, the country was devoid of the century-old prejudices of feudal and ethnically based pathologies. It is true that the United States has not been able to overcome the issue of race. But it is also fair to underline the degree to which civilized views among the dominant majority have attempted to achieve progress for black Americans since World War II. The continuing area of failure in terms of equality of opportunity for black Americans is the result of a complex range of economic, social, and political difficulties. But that lack of progress no longer has official sanction or societal concurrence.

The historical and social forces that combine to produce today's United States are both the product and the cause of the country's economic reality. Economics and social policy are mutually dependent.

Canada is a country whose mix of economic and social realities is not just a product of the economic appeal of a resource-rich economy. During the postwar period Canada's resource-rich economy did produce a huge positive balance of trade which, in fact, helped finance expansions of the social safety net to include such pillars of civility as Medicare. But Canada is also a country where the respect for English and French origins and linguistic and cultural rights, and a larger than most per capita contribution to the war effort, built a nation tied to a sense of both accommodation and, where necessary, sacrifice.

The impetus of American independence may well have been a mercantile and political distaste for badly managed British colonial administration.

The impetus of Canada's confederation was a loyalist preference for order and stability, along with a healthy fear of both the Fenian raids and more straitlaced expressions of post-Civil War American manifest destiny. Canada's Fathers of Confederation had little faith in the midterm civility or passivity of America's continental stance. And, the Civil War had spoken volumes about how the U.S. sorted out its problems — an approach Canadians did not embrace at the time of the American Revolution and were less interested in a century later.

The compelling American values of "life, liberty, and the pursuit of happiness" differ greatly from Canada's equally emblematic constitutional values of "peace, order, and good government." But however they differed, the organizing principles of both societies were never, to the best of my knowledge, replaced with the core values of "prosperity for a few, price stability and job-free economic expansion."

While the Canadian and American views may differ — and may have differed historically for good reason — it is clear that these views of society relate to the organizing principles of how and why people live together, and not to compelling and overriding immutable economic nostrums beside which all else pales by comparison.

But what do we see today? It is one of the emblems of neoconservative excess that important postwar developments in the U.S., whether on race, demographics, civil rights, or social organization, are considered in a narrow economic context of costs, efficiencies, productivity, and yield.

This shortsightedness clearly infects neoconservatism in Canada, where organizing principles of community, changes like the Charter of Rights, or issues like native self-government are similarly appraised solely and narrowly on economic lines. And in both countries the nihilistic and defeatist neoconservative forces, think tanks, and media tilt strongly against anything other than market-driven reality, just in case Americans or Canadians wanted to appraise any developing issues along some broader perspective.

There is no little value in understanding work and economic growth as essential components of our lives as participants in a larger society. But to make the economic components utterly and completely dominant — to make the economic model the only model — is to deny the essence of what freedom and responsibility, combined, provide for the vast majority of our people.

We are not in the years approaching the millennium any less part of or extensions of the organizing principles of our past than were our parents or grandparents. What brought many of them to our shores was a desire for the balance between freedom and responsibility delivered by our societies.

We do not embrace religious intolerance. We are more pluralist than most other societies. We see tolerance of diversity as a good thing. We are troubled about undue exploitation. We grapple with issues of rights and responsibilities. We embrace a free press. We build social infrastructures around values and positive concern. We believe that it meant something — in terms of happiness and cohesion — to be citizens with rights and responsibilities. We believe that a citizen had something to say about how society ran — and something to contribute in support of that society. And while we value self-reliance and independence, we believed that just as citizens came to the aid of their country in times of war, at great human cost, so might their country, or state, or province, or community come to their aid during times of difficulty or need. Whether it was the construction of social security in the United States, or universal health care in Canada, both reflected specific national responses to this relationship with the citizen.

From the end of the nineteenth century through to the reality of postwar social programs, we in North America democratized economic opportunity by making it broadly available. Higher percentages of access to home ownership, medical care, higher education, and economic participation spoke to a belief in the dignity of the human condition, the relationship between rights and responsibilities.

There was a value to home, hearth, family, community labor, study, enterprise, and independence and interdependence that defined how our societies differed from our European and Asian friends. There was a relationship between our quality of life, how we earned that quality, and what it said about the compassion implicit in our way of life.

Let me put my argument this way.

What is the value in terms of costs and outputs of teaching severely handicapped children to feed and dress themselves? What is the measurable output or real economic yield of helping a terminal patient die in comfort and dignity? What is it worth to ensure the ability of public schools to build a real bridge to equality of opportunity? And, at what point in our political debates did it become somehow inappropriate or unaffordable to embrace these and a host of other measures of civility as being of real importance to the decency of our society as a whole?

Can anyone remember actually being invited by any politician of the right or left or center to vote *against* these measures of civility? Can any among us ever remember actually voting to *reduce* the quotient of civility in our society?

Is it not essential to place the economic world, with all its variables and imponderables in some larger context?

There is of course a context that is and must

be about economic pursuits and gains. They are important instruments in a constellation of human and social variables that determine the condition, and the nature, of society.

But to place those instruments at the indisputable *center* of *all* things that matter is to deny the existence of a broader human condition. There is nothing wrong with what participants in financial markets do to create value for their beneficiaries — many of whom are large pension funds and the pensioners to whom they have obligations. But economic concerns are *not* the center of our life as parents, students, farmers, brothers, sisters, or neighbors. Some productive assets in our society do face being financialized by institutional investors who must realize gain for their clients and beneficiaries. But not all.

◆

Sustaining the economic viability of a society requires a focus on critical questions like productivity, skills, cost of capital, and input cost overall. It requires a focus on the mix of skills, conditions, taxation levels, and innovative capacity available for productive enterprise. And productive enterprise can be a huge engine that helps fill the fiscal requirements of a civilized society. In that process, no conservative would dispute that investors have the right to maximize their returns, or that entrepreneurs should face an upside that reflects the downside risks of the investment in time and resources they are making. A country's financial and industrial assets are a significant part of its collective might and capacity.

But that does not mean that its spiritual assets do not matter unless they can be financialized. To do so is to try and place a monetary value on freedom, community, tolerance, pluralism, and the other underpinnings of civility. And to do that is to diminish their underlying values. To do that is to put the right to worship in one's own way, or not at all, on a par, in some way, with this month's increase in the Gross Domestic Product.

And to try and do so is to commoditize the things that matter most. The real determinants of what life is about — love, health, family, opportunity, responsibility, civility, achievement, trust, cooperation, order, and freedom — cannot be measured on any monthly index. The Dow Jones Average, unemployment levels, and housing starts are indicators of but one variable: the economic one. It is compellingly important, but not the center of life and society itself.

Traditional conservatives understand and respect that the most important things in life are beyond simple economic measurement. We understand that excellence, achievement, civility, and stability come more from things of the heart and the soul than as simple outgrowths of enhanced productivity. The instruments of economic achievement are vital components of an economic framework that fills an important place in the hierarchy of successful social organization. But they are means to an end — not an end in and of themselves. They are steps and passageways — not the foundation of the home we share with others in any society.

To break out of the citizen model — where each among us is owed certain protections and in turn owes certain responsibilities to society as a whole — and take refuge in the economic model as the only framework for social definition and community survival is to embrace a determinist and defeatist agenda.

As all local, provincial, or national economic conditions are deeply influenced by global trends, realities, and capital flows, the local, state, or provincial authority can be seen not to matter very much. The will to build or change or improve is only sustainable within the citizen model. As a result, the more this will is diminished by some in the private sector, the less counterbalance to pure economic determinism there is. And that implies a serious distortion of an important balance and equilibrium. Turning means into purposes turns civic priority on its head. And, sadly, it diminishes the importance of the human spirit.

But let us remember that it is the neoconservative who argues for the dominance of the economic model largely because of a core misunderstanding of the connection between citizenship, hope, and stability in feeding economic confidence and social buoyancy.

The tough question is surely not how we survive in growing, expansive, and dynamic economies that provide not only income to finance social justice but also more and more opportunity for all. The question is how we achieve those kinds of societies.

◆

How do we bridge from the economic model, where good employment news in the U.S. generates a sell-off in financial markets because more people working may mean more inflationary wage pressures and the risk of tighter money policies from central bankers, to the human model, where the intrinsic value of more people working productively is a more productive and balanced society?

The first step is to understand that the economic model is an instrument. It is the contractor, the mechanism that citizens use to build towards their goals. Whether citizens are organized into businesses, co-ops, or volunteer groups, or speak through duly elected governments, it is citizens who must use the economic model for their purposes, and not the other way around. The evaporation of the idea that people have choices, and the defeatist attitude that those choices have necessarily been marginalized by forces allegedly beyond anyone's control, is more than serious. It is actually lethal to any measure of social cohesion and stability. It is what the dominance of the economic model leads to: an evaporation of hope. This disappearance of hope, as is the case with far too many in the American inner city, or in the Canadian aboriginal population, leads inexorably to hatred, crime, despair, and division.

When hope evaporates, it leads inexorably to the fearful selfishness, the public and private cynicism, the disregard for the needs and rights of others which the proponents of polarity seek so broadly to exploit. It leads to broad and unsustainable generalizations. If some government is wasteful, then all government is bad. If aspects of some programs in social policy are spendthrift, then all spending in support of social justice is wasteful. If one local government is dishonest, then all in government are corrupt.

This mindless patter becomes the pervasive story line for talk show hosts, neocon columnists, extreme business advocates, and interest group heads. Like waves of red dye, toxic to any form of life with which they come into contact, it forms a thick and opaque layer on the sea of public debate and participation.

And who benefits from this? Certainly not the student working through an education to build her or his place in society. Certainly not the young entrepreneur for whom public confidence and community optimism are vital components. Certainly not the small business person for whom consumer confidence is vital. Certainly not the large corporation, which needs stability in the labor and consumer market — a stability made unsustainable by highly volatile electorates moved by fear, selfishness, cynicism, and the hopelessness of being imprisoned in someone's economic model. Certainly not the volunteer organizations tied to citizen pride and generosity. Certainly not the genuine conservative administration trying, in a state, provincial, or national government, to build linkages that are organic through society as a whole and sustain a genuine balance between freedom and responsibility.

The only winners in this kind of spiritual free fall devoid of moral or uplifting content are the proponents of division who traffic in despondency, polarity, declining spirit, and reduced tolerance, some of whom have done so for decades.

The merchandisers of polarity, too many of whom are found among the neoconservatives, and some of whom are on the far left, are essential to energizing the decline of hope, which is the largest predictor to the end of civility, a precursor to more meaningful collapses in humanity itself.

Unlimited polarity and class division lead to the easy dismissal of opposing views as somehow of lesser value or from lesser people or of causes that are of lesser merit. Neoconservatives are masters at this, belittling the source of any contrary opinion, rather than engaging on the substance of the argument as equals. Their opponents are morally deficient, or insufficiently Christian, or, in the new neocon construct, intellectually somehow more narrow or shallow.

The more traditional conservative view, which seeks not to polarize but to unite, seeks merit in opposing arguments so as to reconcile. It disdains artificial or hyped polarity, because division for its own sake serves no purpose. Conservatism embraces the enterprise-based economic model, but as only one aspect of the larger truth. It does not see polarization as a valid route to electoral victory. And it values cooperation as a sinew of hope not an admission of weakness. Balanced labor/management relations, a capitalism that also embraces employee share ownership, a respect for the right of people to decent paying jobs through which they contribute to society and sustain their own economic needs — none of these fits comfortably into the winner-take-all preferred economic model of the neocons.

What they fail to understand — or worse do understand and don't care about — is the damage to all economic models the end of citizenship will bring. The end of citizenship is the end of stability. The end of citizenship — its subjugation to the indiscriminate forces of some large black macro-economic hole — leads inexorably to the end of civility. The victory of the forces of polarity means the defeat of moderation and common enterprise.

There are no next steps once moderation and common enterprise collapse, and nowhere to go when hope itself — hope for a future of individual and collective achievement — is snuffed out.

That neoconservatives, who actively promote a Darwinian approach to all this, should be untroubled by any of this is, in view of how their movement profits from the merchandising of polarities, unsurprising. That some in the media should be their willing if naive accomplices is, however, truly surprising.

5

The Unwitting Media Allies

Most practitioners in the media world, even those on the thoughtful right and in the tabloid press — not to mention journalists on the left — would be horrified to see themselves as even unwitting instruments of the neoconservative assault on hope in Western society and democracy. Yet the mutual dependencies between the neocon merchandisers of polarity and the solutionist media deepen almost daily in a host of ways.

The solutionist media are the many practitioners who help create and sustain an expectation that the governing process can solve all problems — with solutions deemed, by the media, naturally, and whoever is in opposition at the time, to be easily achievable.

This of course sets aside the hard historical fact in democracies that many policy solutions are themselves the seeds of the next generation of problems.

Some of my friends on the traditional and more moderate right would argue, and not unpersuasively, that this reflects some of the so-called left leanings of many in the press. But, however I might wish it did, this attractive and intuitively appealing proposition simply does not survive any kind of careful analysis. In fact, there are crucial underlying factors here that must be carefully laid out, and they embrace issues far more important than any particular bias that may exist in any particular story.

The most compelling factor is how the media have changed. My concern here is not concentration of media ownership, but rather the passage of many media companies from private or family ownership to ownership by financial and institutional investors through public capital markets. This kind of ownership creates a quarterly pressure for earnings growth and strong margins, an emphasis on reducing costs and increasing the pressure on generating content at the lowest possible cost.

The lower the content cost, the higher the ratio between advertising, subscription revenues, and the costs of overheads. And this rule is as relevant in print media as it is in broadcast, cable, satellite, and digital communications.

Producing an hour of good comedy, good drama, good variety is extremely expensive. Sending a journalist with some genuine expertise to cover an important issue off the beaten track is expensive. What we get instead, and increasingly, is filler masquerading as news and views and substantive content.

A fixed bureau in Washington at the White House, or at Congress, a fixed bureau at the House of Commons in London or Ottawa, or at state or provincial legislatures across the continent can send in all kinds of content daily without any new or added variable costs. And, there are no talent fees to pay beyond base overheads. Politicians, interest groups, opposition leaders, minority leaders, union spokesmen, and lobbyists are delighted to array themselves in front of microphones for little reason and no fee. This is truly a broadcaster's and editor's dream: free content from which to choose, generated at no marginal cost, daily, hourly, every day.

One notices that supper-hour news packages in many major markets in North America have lengthened from the 6:00 to 6:30 slot to run from 5:30 to 7:00. All-news channels have proliferated. And all because the underlying economics are essentially quite compelling and irresistible. The same competitive reality drives the tabloid TV news shows that take up more and more time on daily schedules. The print media's version of this is the use of continuing polls as frequently as possible. When spread over all the papers in the chain — and often split with a TV network in terms of cost — the actual cost per reader is negligible. And a poll — especially on an intrinsically divisive issue like abortion or capital punishment or affirmative action — has the added value not only of being dirt cheap, but also of being likely to generate a reverberating controversy. This allows people to comment on the poll, prompting the media to lay on another level of commentary on other people's comments: all cheap grist for the mill.

The fact that nothing has happened here that remotely resembles "news" is actually neither here nor there. It is the underlying economics that drive the process.

◆

How does this relate to the solutionist bias of the press and the attack on hope? Well, in order to truly advance margins you need audience, and the larger or more demographically defined the audience, the more likely advertisers will pay what one's "cost per thousand" rate card suggests. The more viewers, the more one can charge, especially to those advertisers who need broad and meaningful reach. Content becomes *viewer* driven, not fact driven. The purpose becomes sustaining and growing existing audience bias rather than informing the viewer with facts.

During the time I worked in Ottawa for the prime minister between August of 1991 and April of 1993, a distinguished bureau chief for a national network told me over lunch that one of the reasons his network's coverage of most politicians was somewhat negative was because that's what public opinion wanted and his network needed supper-hour audiences to generate revenue.

While this did not automatically imply contrivance or bias, it did mean that given a choice that showed any government or any politician in a good or bad light, there would be a marked preference for the bad light option, as it was more market sensitive.

One begins to see the solutionist bias, within an anti-elitist "dumbing down" framework, when you add to this the need, especially for television and the tabloid press, and certainly for AM talk radio, which is now a dominant AM presence in North America, to simplify, dealing in good guys and bad guys. Whatever the problem — high taxes, medical system stress, high prices, unemployment, traffic tie-ups, family violence, the insanity of Serbia and Bosnia — government ought to, it is deemed, usually after a question from an opposition spokesperson, have a solution.

The failure to offer a solution is portrayed as an abdication of humanity or compassion or caring.

This is the opposite extreme from the neoconservative assault on hope. It is the media industry's manufacturing of the unsustainable expectation that most serious problems have simple answers.

It exists in a myriad of ways. The columnist who attacks government for not spending more on a social program even when there is no evidence that spending more will help.

The endless search for people to blame when things go wrong — largely because an audience-building story line requires someone to blame.

◆

More pernicious is the cooperation, with the encouragement of the media, of all those who seek government to act so as to deal with problems there is little evidence government can do much about.

The creation of solutionist bias and expectation, which few governments can meet, feeds the general cynicism and discouragement about government overall.

To be fair, politicians often gain office by offering solutionist scenarios themselves. While in office they are easily seduced by media lines of questioning that start with "Mr. Secretary, don't you think your department should be doing more to . . .?"

In Canada, a question to a minister in parliament or provincial legislature is often premised on a preamble that cites new statistics on an issue like family violence or alleged immigration fraud — and has a built-in bias in favor of government possessing, but having heretofore concealed, some new measure or instrument that would solve the problem.

The courage to challenge the solutionist premise is not in abundance, but in some respects it has not yet completely disappeared from realistic people in public life. But the price one pays for it — being typecast by the press as insensitive and unfeeling — is high, a major deterrent to frank talk on tough issues.

The solutionist bias adds two important notes to the neoconservative refrain. Neoconservatives question the relevance of government and collective action on all counts — especially if moderate and incremental. The muscular rhetoric of many neocons prefers simple solutions and views nuance as subversive. They abhor the moderation of incremental public policy, for this lacks the broad sweep and grandeur of the wide application of some compelling exclusionary nostrum that parodies some common truth. Solutionist media bias shares this same impatience.

As well, the solutionist bias implies that simple solutions *do* exist to compelling social and economic problems; hence the notion of complexity is portrayed as an unsustainable political or bureaucratic pretense to prevent remedial action or change. Neoconservatives market their simple solutions to complex problems on the very same pretext. They intellectualize their attack on expertise, experience, and incrementalism. It is the media's game of simplifying most things and earnestly pushing for quick and easy solutions. Clearly, the fact that neoconservative extremes (along with extremes on the left over the years) have marketed this disapproval of complexity may well explain the media's unseemly infatuation with every jot and tittle of the neoconservative journey from inherited cradle to armed stroller over the past few years.

What it does explain, without presuming malice or intent on either side, is the unwitting alliance between neoconservative leadership and solutionist media bias.

Both diminish our collective will to work rationally together, by destroying hope in our society on any issue of common purpose and then by unreasonably raising expectation on a daily basis that cannot possibly be sustained.

This one-two punch, which attacks public morale and spirit, is strengthened by the discovery by both the press and the more extreme neoconservatives, including nativists like Buchanan and solutionists like the parliamentary bureau chief, that news and entertainment are but one and the same. Mr. Perot and his simple life by color charts, the right wing think tanks' debt clocks, the Rush Limbaugh daily cartoon, play into the genre of the tabloid news shows. Interestingly, the American tabloid TV genre began around newsy half hours with journalists sharing earnest trivia about people who really were in showbiz. No one should be surprised that shows were cloned to deal with the political side, in precisely the same genre. Mr. Clinton was not forced to play saxophone on late night TV. He chose to do so, to broaden the reach of his candidacy for the presidency of the United States. Politicians, especially those who have never met a microphone or TV camera they didn't like, contribute to the dumbing down process by facilitating an overexposure that along with most other kinds of excessive familiarity truly breeds contempt. Not all the choices to be made are the media's.

But their approach to the magnification of

dysfunction and the exaggeration of polarity is a choice viewers and readers and advertisers can hold them responsible for, and should.

The tactic of the neoconservative and neoliberal extremist in post-Cold War North America has been to exaggerate massively those areas where things do not work well, while ignoring, and frankly praying others will ignore, what does work.

They have a clear and present interest in advancing public and private pessimism. It has always been my impression that the extreme fundamentalist Christian lobby and the more extreme anti-feminist neoconservative forces had no choice but to kill the Colin Powell candidacy before it left the stable. The election of a black American who was a product of the allegedly dysfunctional public school system, who had spent his life in *honorable public service* (the very term is an oxymoron to neoconservatives), who was a moderate in the Rockefeller tradition, and who believed that including all Americans in the "American Family" was a key premise for public policy — would pose an absolute survival risk to the neoconservative movement itself. That the U.S. was robbed in this last election of a good and decent man to contest and likely win the presidency could not have mattered less to the neocon and fundamentalist Christian right. Powell came to the prospect with his own unbrokered, unlobbied, and incoercible constituency: the American people. Clearly, a popular moderate who had an inclusive and balanced view who began with his own broad constituency had to be stopped. Even moderate and influential conservative voices like William Kristol, who showed constructive interest in the Powell candidacy, could not restrain the zealots' excess.

The optimism about America, about race issues, about public education and public service that Powell's candidacy would have reflected had to be snuffed out by the forces of reaction.

The narrow, nativist, and isolationist excesses of a Pat Buchanan that embarrass even some neoconservatives are premised on a culture of dysfunction, a broad perception that nothing works right.

◆

Canadians may well have found most eerie the similarity between the Buchanan attack on international trade agreements and the consistent attack by Canada's left on those same agreements. The portrayal by both sides of a foreign bogeyman as the agent of dysfunction speaks volumes to where immoderate prescriptions of the right and left usually and inexorably lead.

The media must come to terms with the way in

which their activities and excesses, their abdications and formulaic schedule, feed the universal "myth" of dysfunction.

I do not subscribe to the kind of self-satisfied complacency that simply denies the reality of grinding poverty, global famine, continued unemployment, or crime. But I do take the view that the best way to address these issues, and address them effectively, is to appreciate realistically the relevant facts. Massive media concentration on violent crime — because it is easy and popular to cover and exaggerate and fits the dumbing down formula of TV and print tabloids — does not mean violent crime has increased. Excessive and exaggerated media coverage of personal, stylistic, and allegedly corrupt foibles of elected leaders does not mean that democratic politics are today more corrupt than they were 20, 30, or 50 years ago. Indeed by any rational analysis the opposite is very much the case.

For every high school student in North America involved with drugs there are hundreds who graduate and contribute to their communities and countries and universe. How often do we hear of them? For every product recall, tens of thousands of products are researched, produced, marketed, and sold that provide real value at a fair price every day, to millions of consumers.

Human longevity is increasing. Today's seniors

in North America are by a significant measure more financially independent than previous generations. The collapse of communism and the Cold War's end, while no global or regional panacea, did represent a meaningful victory for Western determination on defence spending in the 1980s. None of this is a pretext for a complacent disregard for problems that must be addressed. But they provide a context, a genuine context within which other problems should be assessed.

The absence of context is the clear condition precedent to successful solutionist or dumbing down media hype. Ahistoric analyses utterly devoid of how we made choices on similar issues in the past are a vital element of talk radio certainty on crucial issues.

Here are a few examples:

In all the media hype about intergenerational tension on wealth and pensions and social security, rarely does anyone look at the decisions taken in the 1960s and 1970s when indigence among the elderly was a serious North American problem. Seniors are not more financially secure by accident. They are secure because of the policy decisions openly taken and widely supported. In the endless focus on government waste, rarely is the government's percentage of expenditures under attack in comparison with excesses, waste, and simple bad management in the private sector — waste that usually, by the way, is subsidized by tax loss allowance in both Canada and the United States.

When a bill or measure dies on the order paper or in conference between the House and the Senate, rarely is there a listing of the ones that have passed effectively.

When a company is found by the media to have violated a labor practice code or environmental regulation, rarely are its many other areas of constructive compliance cited or explained.

When an international agreement unravels — or there is a dispute between two countries on a trade matter — what goes unreported? The thousands of products and services that are exchanged every minute of every hour. This is particularly true of disputes that arise between Canada and the U.S. on trade matters, which rarely reflect more than 1 or 2% of all the trade that goes on. This contextually dishonorable approach helps feed the excessive rhetoric of the Buchanans on America's far right.

For all the genuine difficulties in immigration policy, both Canada and the U.S. are immense beneficiaries of the waves of legal immigration and refugee acceptance over the years. To point to the strength, investment, vigor, energy, and motivation brought to our shores does not create licence to ignore illegal immigration scams. But an out of context focus only on illegal aliens plays into the hands of bigoted xenophobic and extreme groups, who thrive desperately on this sort of "find some-one else to blame" politics of polarity. From Ross Perot in the United States, to Mr. Buchanan in the early primaries, to Preston Manning's early Reform days in Canada's west, to ousted separatist Premier Parizeau in Quebec — one often finds an implicit appeal to intolerance as the prime beneficiary of this bad immigration mythology.

The steps to a collapse in public confidence and collective lie all around us.

Destroy hope or the ability of democracy to succeed at anything. Create pessimism about public service, elected or otherwise. Increase expectations and appetite for nonexistent solutions. Dumb down all issues to the most pejorative possible view of their dynamics.

Operate in response to the public's prejudices and misconceptions. Feed them, exploit them. Market to and through them. Build audience based on black and white options. Increase focus on minutia. *Never* use any context or relevant history when pursuing a contemporary setback. Overstate the negative. Ignore or understate the positive. Never leave out the entertaining, the trivial, the personal. Overexpose those who fail. Diminish those who work effectively, especially in the common good.

That this list exists or reflects so easily how both neoconservatives and their unwitting allies in the media contribute to the end of both civility and politics in a democracy should surprise few careful observers.

That the media, for reasons that are internally and systemically driven, should be such effective if unwitting accomplices to the marauding, more extreme, neoconservative attack on public hope and optimism is what should be most troubling.

In fact, I am prevented from seeing the entire industry as unindicted co-conspirators with the neoconservative merchandisers of polarity only because of my good fortune to know many able and thoughtful people in the media who are deeply troubled by the effect of broad stroke populist hokum on public policy issues.

But succumbing to that temptation — however attractive — would be to be excessively pessimistic and ignorant of the broader truth that many men and women in journalism in Canada and the U.S. clearly do try to avoid these excesses, in a fashion that speaks to their professionalism and balance.

So it is not all bad. There are redeeming moments, events and patterns of courage. But there are not enough. And the price society pays for this in terms of balance and hope is distressingly high.

6

Hating Government from the Inside

The destruction of hope — the dilution of any sense of utility, collective will, or common purpose — emanates from many sources. The exigencies tied to international capital mobility and the local impacts of competitive labor cost factors underlying global investment decisions — all, especially when misrepresented, can contribute to a feeling of helplessness and a sense that national government means less. The porous media world, in which imagery and information permeate all political boundaries, also contributes to a diminishing sense of national autonomy or local political relevance.

But these forces, in and of themselves, are benign in the larger context of the destruction of hope.

Delaying or avoiding free trade would only have increased the core inefficiency of domestically protected monopolies, to the long-term detriment of workers and taxpayers, citizens and consumers. Countries that indulged themselves this way would simply have fallen prey to weakening trade balances, collapsing currencies, and collapsing standards of living.

Eastern European countries faced the collapse of their living standard and radical currency inflation not because they opened their borders to the world but because of the gap between their lengthy enslavement to command control economics and their new economic freedoms. It was of course essential to totalitarian communism to prevent permeable economic borders. But the cost of this economic isolation from the real world in relative efficiency and competitive standing for the Eastern European worker has been immense. It is not surprising that those countries that were more open sooner in the postwar years, like Czechoslovakia, Poland, Hungary, and Estonia, are now better able to offer their citizens genuine opportunities for economic betterment. Any dismissal of economic forces as all bad or all dehumanizing — a canard we hear often from the left — is both excessive and without substance. The forces themselves are neutral. How we handle them, how we deal with their impact and channel them, is what matters.

The same can be said of international media penetration on a global basis. Some have offered the view that the inevitability of *glasnost* and *perestroika* was heightened by the penetration of Western media imagery through Eastern European television sets. The absence of same in the Peoples' Republic of China is said to be a clear benefit for Chinese authorities seeking to avoid democratization and political liberalization.

In the end, with respect to the Soviet Union, the common commitment of the NATO alliance to match and exceed Soviet defence spending, the rise of legitimate dissidents, and economic aspiration at the personal and community level all conspired to make Gorbachev's task of questioning communist orthodoxy the reflection of an unavoidable economic reality — as opposed to a fresh creation. But his courage in questioning the long march of five-year plans and Soviet expansionism was the catalyst that focused the Soviet people on other ways of governing and managing their lives.

This was no move from the left to the right. It is, and was, a move from the unworkable to the workable. Those on the right who believe the scoreboard at the dissolution of the USSR was capitalism 1, communism 0 are awash in a sea of self-delusion. And those who expound that the demise of one untenable system automatically means the strengthening of the competing system are equally deluded.

The reality is that the weaknesses of the Soviet system were not and are not reverse images of our many strengths. The collapse of one building, improperly engineered from the outset and badly maintained, does not necessarily mean that other buildings that have not collapsed are utterly without structural flaw.

And one of the structural flaws we face is the government-hating agenda, which has been with us, really, since Watergate, advanced both willfully and unwittingly by people and events in the quarter-century since.

Nixon's inability to admit White House misdeeds, cut his losses, and let the chips fall where they should have early on afforded the U.S. and the world a glimpse of how power might, on occasion, not be held as a trust in the public interest but be used other ways.

More media focus on the excesses of the Kennedy period in government, in terms of nepotism, proximity to organized crime, ballot stuffing, favoritism, and the rest, would have produced this awareness a decade earlier, and perhaps in a more gradual way.

Carter's amiable and progressive incompetence only added to the sense that government in the U.S. was about other people who worked in ways so different from the ways in which average Americans were held accountable. Nixon's contribution to a sense of deconstruction was both willful and unwitting. Carter's was clearly rooted in the populist everyman aspiration he could ignite electorally — but could not deliver on in government.

The Reagan era is in a sense more clear. As Garry Wills, one of America's most thoughtful, popular, and balanced conservative historians and writers, wrote of Reagan's era on the eve of the most recent Republican presidential convention, "There was a real animus against even diminished government action; a hatred of one's own tools . . . Washington has become the *fons et origo* of all that is wrong with the country. That attitude was fostered by Reagan as he voiced from the inmost center of government a low regard for governing. . . . Conservatives have for decades been concerned about 'subversions' in government. But the real subverters of our government were the ones who worked in and against it at the same time, acting from a disloyalty they could not openly express . . ." *

---

* "Reagan Country," *The New York Times Magazine*, August 11, 1996.

As Wills pointed out, it is Dick Armey, key Republican strategist in the Contract with American congressional battle, who likened those who attempted new frontiers, great societies, and new deals to the perpetrators of Soviet and Chinese five-year plans and great leaps forward.

It is the disavowal of nuance and particularity here that is so destructive. Those who attempted the New Deal, the Great Frontier, or the Great Society — programs over which any thoughtful conservative would worry, in terms of the corrosive effect unreachable expectations would have on the public — did so in democratic, partisan, and competitive political context. Simply issuing edicts from the politbureau is not similar in any way.

If failure at all intended goals and purposes — or the risk of failure in some measure — were to determine how rational people lived their lives, no one would ever start a business, design a building, paint a picture, or start a school year.

Because some measures attempted by government are wasteful or inefficient or less than successful is no reason to oppose all government.

On that basis — and this is absolutely essential to the fundamental difference between traditional conservatives and the neoconservatives — one would surrender all the tools collectively available for order and stability, along with the collective will, simply because there has been program failure in the past. Tools of government should be used sparingly, and the state should defer when community, family, and private sector options can sort out areas without government presence. This should be a majority of the time, but the hard truth is that in areas of order, stability, democratic process, fairness, and social justice, there is a role that government should and can play. Surrendering that option, as neoconservatives so eagerly do, is worse than a hostage taking. It is the process in which we actually volunteer to be the hostages, held captive by a fate that is beyond any rational understanding. Some, who argue for the surrendering of these tools of common will, argue that any interference with the market is a clear economic threat to everyone's long-term interests. Traditional conservatives disagree. The majesty of free markets is their defiance of predictable plans established by those who participate in them. That is the essence of risk, and why those who take risks in the free-market system deserve fair reward. But market majesty does not extend to preserving order, or strengthening the instruments of genuine equality of opportunity.

And here lie the core risks produced by extreme neoconservative deconstructionism and hatred of government. And the agenda is pervasive.

In Canada, those in the Reform party who would move away from public funding for aspects of inter-regional equalization, those who would remove the state from core competencies, have obviously learned little from what a deconstructionist agenda can do and is doing in the U.S. That mainline Conservatives like Premier Harris of Ontario or Premiers Klein or Filmon in Alberta and Manitoba hold fast to core principles of civility like public education, universal health care, or core welfare levels speaks to a sensibility shaped by more traditional conservative concerns about social stability and justice.

It is not too much to ask those who run for office to have a plan for how that office may be and should be used in the public interest and to propose how that may happen. They may wish to reduce the office's cost. They may seek a mandate to change its mission. They may wish to execute the office's responsibilities in different ways — ways that use less government apparatus, for example, and bring in more private sector or community leverage. All of this makes sense. But to run for office without having any belief in the potential efficacy of government in any way is to be part of a political bait and switch of the worst order.

Reagan produced the worst deficit in American history. The gap between rich and poor widened.

The permanent underclass grew in numbers and despair. How does that advance the reach and relevance of free enterprise? How does that assist the stability and potential of capital markets?

As in the Nixon and Carter administration — which can list the end of the Vietnam War, the opening to China, the Israeli-Egyptian Peace Accord as their achievements — so too were there serious achievements during the Reagan era, in both foreign and domestic policy. But the unreeling of the deconstructionist agenda, in America and beyond, is simply not one of them.

The governments we are being encouraged by the extremes to hate are not militarily imposed or sustained by dictatorial rule. They are governments elected by us. And while we may well on occasion want to throw the rascals out, hating government in the way some neoconservatives seem to relish is a fairly large piece of hating ourselves. The democratic processes we all face on *both* sides of the border are not without built-in structural and systemic problems. But they are eminently more fair and open than most systems elsewhere. There are issues of transparency that can and must be addressed. But the inequities are no reason to dismiss the outcome or the process.

Government is the reflection of those concerns we all have beyond the level of community, family, and neighborhood. It is the expression of who we think we are at the municipal, state, provincial, or federal levels. It is the reflection of our transient consensus, at any one time, on issues, priorities, and electoral choices. It is the institutional framework, the orderly infrastructure for addressing conflicting interests and societal needs. It is the countervail, when necessary, to large corporate or union interests, when and if they become abusive.

Above all, governments are the permanent and transient expression of the public interest. The permanent expression is the body of laws and institutions we inherit and which evolve over time. The transients are the political leaders and parties we entrust temporarily with political control on our behalf.

But more important than all this is the assertion that there *is* a *public interest*, common to the population as a whole, and there are, however imperfect, defenders of that interest, proponents and arbiters who are accountable under the law to the rest of us for the decisions they make. A vibrant democracy provides no end of debate about that public interest, no end of controversy about what it is and how it is discharged — which is precisely what democracy is about.

The notion, however, that by hating government from the inside, and encouraging widespread cynicism about it one advances the public interest is similar to suggesting that by reducing the costs of a hockey team by removing the goalie, you enhance your chances of winning.

There is a competitive tension, a match of wits and intellect, between elected authorities and competing interests which while legitimate are not broadly elected or accountable. And just as unions, foreign companies, domestic industries, speculators, and interest groups have every right to advance their respective causes, so does the population as a whole have a right to have their collective interest — the public interest — advanced and asserted and promoted by responsible and accountable governments.

The proponents of the public interest may not always be right on any given issue, but they have the responsibility to have a view. This is not about overarching or overreaching government. It is about a dynamic reference point for the public interest as an important presence in any democratic society.

Canada's size, scope, expenditures, and biases are open always for public debate and redesign through our democratic process. But diluting that process down to being of no consequence is simply to accept the neoconservative shibboleth that there is no public interest.

And to do that is to negate democracy itself.

7

Confronting the Gospel of Division

Understanding the old and new left roots of much of neoconservatism's earliest founding fathers like Irving Kristol or Michael Novak helps one understand the gospel of division that the new right so profoundly espouses.

I remember as a student on campus in the late '60s at the University of Ottawa how the left loved to divide and redivide the world. Not even communists were safe. There were Trotskyites, Marxist-Leninists, Maoists, and the odd Bolsheviks. When they ran for parliament, they would list the kind of communists they were: Communist party (Marxist-Leninist), as if the parenthetical detail would clearly put them over the top. Those were the days when to be in student government as a conservative was of such a rarity that any notion of different varieties here was both futile and irrelevant.

In Canadian politics, this virus of the left infected the New Democrats, who had evolved honorably from the old Co-operative Commonwealth Federation. By the mid-'70s, a hard left "Waffle" contingent was dividing the New Democratic party and fielding its new leadership candidate (James Laxer), who gave the more centrist party establishment a good run for their money.

(To be fair here, dissension did not just exist in the NDP. After the 1974 federal election, when NDP leader David Lewis stepped down, tributes were paid from all sides in the House of Commons. Conservative leader and former Nova Scotia premier Robert Stanfield, whose federal political career was halted in part by the center-left defacto coalition between Lewis and Liberal leader Pierre Trudeau, rose to assure Mr. Lewis that he need not lament dissent in his party. "In your party," I recall Stanfield as saying, "the dissidents are called the Waffle. In Mr. Trudeau's party they are called the cabinet. In mine they are called the membership.")

But the left's ability to divide and subdivide based on everything from race to ethnicity, from tax bracket to gender, is one of their enduring and most compelling weaknesses.

It is difficult to advance the oppressed if you are not prepared to identify precisely who they are. Hence the subgroups, such as fem-lib, left-green, gay-lib, enviro-lib, etc. Don't get me wrong. All individuals have the right to assume whatever political identity they choose, and to lawfully advance it as a cause or a platform if that is their wish. It has simply never struck me as a terribly effective tool for public persuasion or broadening the base.

But until the advent of neoconservative swagger and excess, until those who had as American liberals trained their guns on communist world conspiracies decided to train them on American public institutions and public policy, we had not seen the old division-centered view of the world cross the tracks to the conservative side of the street.

In the U.S., old style conservatives believed in a people's "oneness" under G-d. Some believed in oppressive establishments that were anything but progressive on issues like race or economic fairness; some believed, as Teddy Roosevelt did, in the people's rights over the rights of the "trusts" that centralized economic and business power excessively.

Conservatives in the U.K., from Disraeli to Churchill, may not have been as devoted to the eradication of tradition as their Labourite opponents, but they always sought to soften the material class distinctions in support of the sovereignty of the British people, usually under the Nation and Enterprise and One Britain banner.

In Canada, Conservative parties from Sir John A. Macdonald, the first prime minister, to John Diefenbaker, who led the nation's government into the 1960s, always sought to reach out and broaden the party and its message beyond its traditional demographic. Diefenbaker especially spoke out against the idea of the hyphenated Canadian. He sought, in the British tradition of One Nation conservatives, to encourage those who brought to Canada strong ethnic identities from the Old Country to sustain a broad pan-Canadian identity by which cultural pride was integrated with an unhyphenated Canadian citizenship for all.

For better or worse, English-speaking conservatism in the U.S., Canada, and the U.K. sought to bring people together, in what they saw as the right cause.

What the neocons brought to the movement was the culture of division. There was Christian conservatism, and Christian America, against the godless and the heathen. There was the culture of the oppressed and badly treated white male. There was the attack on those in the public service. There was the attack on immigrants. There was the classification of crimes by color. There was the supremacy of the stay-at-home mother versus other women. There were those who produced economic growth and those who were burdens on the state. There were the pointy-headed northeastern eggheads versus the clear-thinking southwesterners. And, oh yes, true to the intensity of the convert, the liberals they deserted to become neoconservatives were open to a special range of divisive attacks and vilifications.

Lots of new enemy lists here! University professors, New Yorkers, civil rights and native rights activists, school boards opposed to censorship, and anyone who had ever dared to believe that black Americans, many of whom still live in inner city societies with all the attributes of some third world countries, might, just might, benefit from a helping hand — all were lumped together in a rogue's gallery of affirmative action villains.

The culture of division became not just the gospel of the new right but its overarching and core tactic and strategy. Getting people not to see themselves as "fellow Americans" but as better Americans, Americans being held back by welfare moms, or black activists, or proponents of contrary views was key to the tactic of divide and conquer. No longer was disagreement about the purposes of government simply that: disagreements reflecting the pluralism of democracy. Disagreement with the one true way — the neoconservative path that uncoupled social justice from economic growth — meant only that such disagreement had to come from those who had a vested interest in a society of mediocrity or the lowest common denominator.

This divisive strategy fueled the attack on public schools, the attack on health insurance, the attack on government generally and social programs in particular. It fueled the attack on public housing and welfare.

A few outstanding Republicans took a more inclusive and purposefully less divisive approach over the years, like Bill Scranton of Pennsylvania, Romney and Milikan of Michigan, Rockefeller and Bush in their vice presidential and presidential or putative presidential roles. Jack Kemp is rightfully distinguished by his consistent desire to sweep disadvantaged Americans into the economic mainstream.

But battling against some of these were the Podhoretz-Kristol crowd (the fathers, not the sons), the Christian right, and a host of massively overfunded foundations that produced paper after paper and conference after conference extolling the virtues of an ever more consistent division of Americans into winners and losers — within, of course, the neoconservative framework of a winner-take-all world.

◆

To recoil from this divisive ideology is not to embrace the politics of the lowest common denominator. It is to embrace the inherently conservative politics of equality of opportunity.

The traditional conservative opposition to transcendent liberalism and to utopian socialism comes from the disconnect from reality of these two profound misunderstandings of human nature. Classical liberalism, the true and utterly vapid origin of today's neocon eccentricities, is the naive worship of both the individual and human nature. Stemming from a profound dislike of the authoritarianism of the theocratic church-controlled and monarchical states, this approach exalted the view that, left on its own, human nature was a wonderful thing, incapable of cruelty or deceit and utterly confirming of the great potential of the individual. Just leave people alone, remove all structure, laws, controls and constraints, and everyone will just do fine. This is the core conceit of laissez-faire.

As is often the case with excess, the root idea — of reducing unfair and narrow authority somewhat and encouraging more freedom and less state- or church-run serfdom — is not bad. However, when you take it to excess, it becomes a philosophy that imposes one new tyranny where an old one existed. The tyranny of the individual, the tyranny of a society without any order or structure or common purpose, is really little more than a hunting licence in today's world for those with inherited wealth or huge corporate strength. Their prey? The inter-generationally poor, the disadvantaged, the old, the young, the small entrepreneur, the farmer, the independent business person. And, besides, beyond the challenges of today it is hard to look back in history at least in modern times and find circumstances where trusting utterly in human nature and removing the constraints of civilization have done much for more than a few.

This neocon obsession with old world liberal laissez faire excess, however, does have to compete for the stupid award with our utopian socialist friends. I have always tended to be less inflamed at my socialist friends despite the wrongness of their views, because their purposes struck me as more noble than those of the laissez faire liberal, and because they at least offered a cohesive vision, however wrong, of how individuals should relate to each other in a society. Liberalism is devoid of any such consideration. But it is here that my tolerance evaporates. While noble enough, "from each according to his ability to each according to their need" fails to address the key point of distribution. Who decides? Is it the local commune? Is it the local state or national committee? This is but one central flaw in the utopian message. There are others.

In the same way that believing that human nature left on its own is always kind, gentle, inspiring, considerate, and law abiding is the worst of naiveté, so too is the belief that removing any hope of personal gain or benefit from people's own effort, hard work, skill set and risk taking, can in any way be inspiring.

Excess on the side of collectivism is as disconnected from the realities of human nature as are excesses on the side of individualism! The classically liberal laissez faire excess (now adopted by neocons as their own) understates profoundly the role of order and social balance. The socialist excess utterly disregards the personal need for benefit from one's own hard work.

Both also depend almost completely on the politics of division to advance their cause.

For socialists, it is about class divisions: trying to create enemies between sources of capital and sources of labor. Dividing the community between "working people" and everyone else. Lately, in the last half-century, divisions have been parsed again and again, ultimately weakening the left with its own brand of quite silly exclusivities.

And the neocons know instinctively that their enemy is any pervasive sense of oneness or community where people actually feel some sense of responsibility to each other, and, in the case of those much weaker through no fault of their own, a responsibility for each other.

The proponents of no government to speak of, the essential eradication of gun laws and most taxes, the imposition of pro-life and Christian fundamentalist fiat, the de-integration of schools, and the end of the public school system cannot survive in an atmosphere of community. They must divide white from black, rich from poor, old from young. They must promote intergenerational and interracial tension — or at least allow it to fester. They must destroy faith in public policy and public office holders.

They must feed off interregional and intergenerational angst, stirring it up whenever they can.

They depend on the corrosive force of division to sustain their politics of beggar thy neighbor small-mindedness. Only in that framework can the selfish option appear sane and appropriate.

If no one or no government or no neighbor can really ever be trusted, well isn't selfishness and withdrawal the only option?

Their logic is impeccable. It is a new gospel that speaks to the worst of the human condition, and ignores all the rest. And when widely enough shared and believed, it is, like most gospels, self-fulfilling.

But it can be stopped.

8

Beyond Division to Community

It has always struck me that the essence of the neoconservative myopia about society comes from the tendency of its staunchest advocates to constantly view the world in terms of "us" and "them," "we" and "they."

It is inherent in their social and political analysis. *We* profit through hard work, risk taking, and determination. *They* are slovenly, lazy, and delighted to live off the dole. *We* work hard and pay too much taxes. *They* are lazy government employees who live off, indeed sponge off, *our* hard work. *We* want our neighborhoods to be clean and safe. *They* want to invade, rob, and disrupt *our* neighborhood. In the hothouse of New York City, liberalism turned neocon evangelical: *we* became liberal Jews and *they* became unappreciative blacks. *We* were the businesses that flowed millions to the right wing foundations in the 1970s and '80s to counter *they* who held different views and had far too much influence.

The problem is not that the "we" and the "they" are always false dichotomies; there are different points of view and competing interests in any society. The challenge in a democracy is what to do about them.

Neoconservatives clearly believe true believer/infidel analysis. The first generation Kristol-Podhoretz-Decter neocon beachhead crew clearly believed that they, having converted from old style squishy liberalism themselves, had a duty to simply convince others to do the same. No bridge building here. No narrowing of gaps. If one has a superior idea or analysis, one just swarms the other side with it until they surrender. For the ubiquitous new right one just gathers enough money, enough publications, enough politicians, fund enough Political Action Committees or foundations and off you go. It is about winning and persuading, not building any kind of common ground.

They fail to understand, along with their disciples and acolytes, that the real barrier between them and the larger population is the same barrier that divides and divided the far left from the public at large. The clear lack of any sense of compromise, of any notion that their certainty might in any way be diluted or changed by the more moderate view of the population as a whole, is in itself a serious constraint on their persuasive reach.

People will tend to view as extreme any positions they cannot relate to or on which they have no impact.

The other darker side of the we-they part of analysis is the degree to which when someone is no longer part of your definition of the mainstream, he or she can be dehumanized and diminished as to their relevance or importance.

The poor are not, in this analysis, potentially comfortable people who have had bad luck or unfair disadvantage; they are simply the poor, and unlike us, even if "us" includes people whose relative success is the result of inheritance.

The people at the public trough are not public servants who raise families, pay bills *and* taxes, and have the same career aspirations and economic needs as anyone else, but simply people at the public trough.

It was interesting to see the price paid recently in the U.S., when the Contract with America crowd in the Gingrich Congress shut down the government. Not only did the media portray what was happening to U.S. citizens with mortgages and rent to pay who happened to work in a government agency, but the impasse revivified what had been to that point a moribund and increasingly irrelevant Clinton presidency. This was a superb example of what happens to neocon excess when it is, as it usually is, utterly disconnected from the day to day reality of the vast majority of people. That it gives voice to frustration and anger and, on occasion, conviction, is not without merit. On its own, however, this is not enough to establish more than a beachhead in the marketplace of ideas.

Because the marketplace of ideas is a reflection of the community as a whole. And to be relevant and motivating, any proposal must not only be instructive, it must also be relevant to and reflective of how real people live, rich and poor, black and white, godfearing and agnostic, optimistic and fatalistic.

My late mother believed that there was no situation that was helped by bad manners or pessimism. But that does not allow me to write off people who are rude and inherently condescending. They, too, have the right to be heard and counted in.

It is incumbent on those who offer prescriptions to the community to embrace a definition of community that is itself all-embracing.

I am reminded of a story told by Martin Connel at a meeting last spring in Toronto. Martin is a leading Canadian businessman who used his business success to start the Calmeadow Foundation, which provides small loans around the world to people who need the money to bootstrap themselves out of poverty. The foundation has been active in the third world and in economically depressed areas of eastern Canada's maritime provinces. Martin also was the moving force behind the "Imagine" campaign, which successfully motivated and involved a host of major companies in supporting charitable and community endeavors.

Martin was relating how, when meeting with fellow senior business leaders on a charitable project, one among them asked him, "Who, by your definition, are the needy we're talking about here?"

Martin paused and said, "Well, actually, it's you and me!"

"How do you mean?"

"Very simply, each of us is perhaps one or two events away from being in that category. If you had a severe car accident and needed both hospitalization and long-term rehabilitation, or if you began to show the symptoms of Alzheimer's disease, or if your wife had a stroke and was paralyzed for some time — you would, however well you may be insured, soon be in need of support from one or another charitable, government, United Way, or other community agency. Each one of us is only one or two events away from being needy."

This is perhaps the most compelling problem the neocons face — unless of course they are content to formulate policy for the super rich, be funded by the super rich to do so, and simply accept that they have little to offer the other 98% of the population.

Public policy need not always underline everyone's vulnerability, but it cannot be shaped on the assumption of invulnerability; that simply denies the harsh and compelling reality of the human condition. In the end, most people do worry about family, health, safety, and the quality of local education and social facilities, because at some point in life they or someone they care about will need them.

◆

It is on this issue of community and its essential role in society that traditional conservatives break utterly from the neoconservative insurgents.

The community, whether it is expressed through volunteer activity in the contexts of recreation, sports, health care, or youth, or in the broader context of institutionalized mandates like universities or hospital boards, is the combination of these absolutely essential expressions of our mutual common interest in shared benefit and experience. Community does what individuals cannot achieve on their own — and often what government cannot do as well.

It is the antithesis of the politics of division.

When churches and synagogues, which are, after all, organizations established, as most charities are, along religious and sectarian lines, open their basements and kitchens to the poor or the homeless, without regard to sectarian concern, that is the antithesis of division.

When parents of all economic and educational backgrounds sell oranges or run bingos so the local swim team can waive dues or swim meet costs for the less advantaged, that is community and not division.

When cereal companies and local volunteers and foundations and school boards come together with government to sponsor a breakfast program, that is community and not division.

Paleo-conservatives like I (now called Red Tories in Canada, Rockefeller Republicans in the U.S., and "Wets" in post-Thatcher Britain) have always seen the structures of the larger community — church, the military, the state — as the sinews of order. In like manner we have seen order as the only possible framework for freedom of any kind. Classical liberalism reversed the hierarchy, putting the individual's prerogatives and human nature well ahead of any structural responsibilities to community. It is no great wonder that neoconservatives who grow from classically liberal roots would miss the importance of community today, and have great difficulty relating to it without seeing some seething collectivist plot.

In democracy, any institution is truly either a product of community or a product of community consensus. That community may be described nationally, locally, vertically, or horizontally. But it is a key part of the cohesion that sustains any kind of social consensus.

For traditional conservatives like I the rights and freedoms of individuals balance with their responsibilities to community and society as a whole — including those with whom they may disagree or whose interests are inimical to their own.

And, conversely, a society's duties to each of its members in return must be executed with equal balance, regardless of the politics of the day or the partisan preferences of the government in power. It is fundamental to a moderate democracy that government's duty to those who voted against it be precisely the same as its duty to those who voted for it, no less and no more.

It is vital that public policy be shaped always with this communitarian principle in mind. It is also vital that the framework for public policy be a mix between guiding convictions and principles on the one hand and community reality and requirement on the other. As a conservative, I am profoundly more optimistic about the capacity of local, state, and provincial government to get this mix right, than central governments that are farther away and, by definition, more remote. Which is not to say that there are not some national community realities that do not require national leadership, as in monetary, defence, or foreign policy, to name a few. But these macro areas should be the exception. National governments are at their most effective when their agenda is compact and they manage it well. Overreaching agendas that defy competent management simply help destroy the franchise of government overall and, to some extent, the legitimacy of community-wide responses to problems or opportunities.

Moving beyond the politics of division and its supporting culture is to leave both the extremes of neoconservatism and socialism to talk among themselves while the rest of civilization attempts genuine progress on real issues and challenges.

Whether it is the regional paranoia of the Canadian Reform party, the nativist and isolationist rhetoric of the Buchanan wing of the Republicans, the divisive self-serving arrogance of the Christian right, or the "smaller Britain" paranoia of the Eurosceptics who haunted and diluted the Major government in the U.K., all share a common thematic bias.

Political traction is achieved, by them, through the politics of division and sometimes fear. It is almost always pitched, as in the approach of Le Pen in France, against some group or groups. It is tied irrevocably to the we-they brand of neoconservative, often fundamentalist, excess. And, because it is self-feeding, it produces the enmity from the "theys" that help sustain their divisive culture.

It has nothing to do with the conservatism that embraces community, reaching out with a message of common purpose and common cause.

It has even less to do with the primary conservative purpose of bringing people together.

9

Making the Case for Community

There can be no more urgent conservative mission than making the case for community. In a sense, the survival of a conservatism of compassion and tolerance, within the framework of societies of enterprise and excellence, is utterly tied to the ability Americans and Canadians have to view themselves, their families, and their enterprises as part of ever-concentric circles of community.

Individual conservatives will have their own experiences to bring to this task. Experiences in the United States will be different from those in Canada. Regional experiences will differ widely. But the definition and defence of community is a central instrument by which the forces of pessimism and division can be contained, and the damage they create diminished.

What exactly do I mean when I talk about community?

In the most direct terms possible, community is the embodiment of the common interest we share with others. The reach and embrace we offer others reflects the range and breadth of our definition of community.

There is a progression here, from the closest and most local to the farthest flung. One's family, one's neighborhood, one's local community are clearly at the foundation of any definition of community. But a foundation without a superstructure does not provide much shelter and provides even less elevation. The strength of the foundation, how well it is built and designed, is essential to the survival of the superstructure, but in and of itself it does not get you very far.

One of my core disputes with many neoconservatives is with their desire to take such a narrow view of community — in sectarian and local terms — that they really seem to prefer living in the basement. I'm delighted to let them have the basement. I don't know why, however, the rest of us should have to crowd in there with them.

It is what one builds on the foundation that determines what one's true quality of life and experience is. Will there be sufficient elevation to see far and wide? Will there be room enough for all? Will there be different rooms of different sizes? Will the structure's systems, like plumbing, heating, and ventilation, work? Will there be communication and interaction? Will there be the ability to help those in need? Will there be room for new arrivals? Will there be linkages with other superstructures elsewhere? Is the superstructure of community that is being built sustainable and affordable? Is it adaptable? Is it reflective of the views of more than those who live in the basement? Is it strong enough to withstand the elements and economic swings? Is it self-financing? Is it able to grow and encourage growth?

These are the key structural questions around the definition of community that conservatives and citizens of all or no political preferences must face. Together they are, in my view, the central issue of the shape and purpose of society, social progress, and the next stages of civilization. To abdicate from this debate is to absent oneself from the central issue of our times. For example:

(1) The continued expansion of economic activity, trade flows, investment and financial markets reflects not only an interdependence between communities but also a core opportunity to finance

social and community progress through the profits, taxes, and community infrastructure that can emerge from this cycle of growth.

There are costs to the unskilled and disadvantaged in this cycle. Industries implode and are restructured. Technologies reduce the need for traditional forms of labor. Mobility of investment and managers and entrepreneurs redefines the old nostrums of the nation state and national sovereignty.

A community view of this phenomenon implies a genuine effort to broaden corporate and social responsibility so as to diminish the number of people left out of the economic mainstream. A traditional conservative view amplifies this to find ways to broaden the economic mainstream so that more workers are shareholders, so that basic income security programs protect the innocent from unmanageable income collapse. A traditional conservative approach looks for the marrying of Nation and Enterprise or social responsibility with economic expansion and genuine profitability.

The classic neoconservative winner-take-all bias sees social responsibility and community as undue burdens on investment and productivity, rather than as essential ingredients in the recipe that encourages both. They would rather live in the basement. Traditional conservatives want to start framing in the infrastructure of a larger society.

(2) Although life in Canada and the United States is devoid of the violence of war, wars rage across the globe, in some ways encouraged by the end of the bipolar world and the liberation both of Soviet client states and the West's satellite systems of countervailing countries. For those who are smug in their good fortune within the foundation of family, neighborhood, and local community, this is a prime time to reduce defence expenditures, refuse to pay U.N. fees (as the U.S. has done since the Reagan era), and tend exclusively to the basement issues of lower taxes and more police.

Sadly, this has made the U.S., since Bush's defeat, somewhat introverted and aloof.

Traditional conservatives send their forces to fight through food aid to Ethiopia, or Somalia, because the definition of community does not exclude those in the most vulnerable and most exposed part of the mansion. In the end, leaving suffering to fester and feed upon itself is simply inviting disaster that can lead right back to the foundation itself. These measures are never easy or without risk. But they are essential. Look at the human price of Europe's dithering on what emerged from the old Yugoslavia. Where would the middle east be today without U.N. and U.S. involvement? What have we gained by America's refusal to consider the people of Cuba as members of a hemispheric community?

One's grasp should exceed one's reach if the goal is a definition of community that expands on the values that form the foundation of one's society. Failure to advance those values or defend them beyond the frontiers of home only brings closer the day when those values will be endangered at home.

If a withdrawal from Africa produced a collapse in some parts of that continent into chaos, crime, and disease, the migratory patterns and the movement of disease would within years, not decades, begin to affect the nations of the West.

Disengagement from the middle east could produce a multidirectional military, nuclear, and terrorist menace that could stop Western enterprise around the globe.

Disengagement from Central and South America could see a culture of drugs, corruption, and murder squads swamp the promising economies and democracies of the region, producing core instabilities for world mining, resource, tourist, and manufacturing economies. Turning a blind eye to the crushing of democracy in parts of Asia only seeds the clouds for more serious confrontation and crises in the future.

(3) There is a genuine risk of a generational limitation to the definition of community particularly as a result of the cult of divisiveness neoconservatives advance. They appeal to seniors by seeking tax cuts and reduction of welfare and expenditures on public education. They appeal to younger people by proposing cuts to seniors' entitlements, social security, and public pensions. Having already set out to sow despair in terms of the future viability of safety net programs, they seek to goad each age group to define community in a chronologically exclusive way.

Traditional conservatives are opposed to warehousing generations separately from each other when the issue of community is addressed. Grandparents and grandchildren may be chronologically different but they share common interests, like safe neighborhoods that lead to investments and jobs. They share a common interest in health care that works for the aged and the newborn. They share an interest in a system that does not unfairly tax savings and wealth while unfairly dispossessing public education and vocational training. They have an interest, a compelling interest, in young people finding productive work so that they can be financially independent as soon as reasonably possible.

They are critical parts of each other's community. They are one community. The traditional conservative works to bring that community together to work out common problems and increase common opportunities.

None of this takes place or needs take place, as neoconservatives would worry, at the cost of personal freedom. If you see personal freedom as a value that exists in a vacuum unrelated to the vagaries of life, this isolationist stance will breed the paranoia of a subsequent and derivative position.

But if as a traditional conservative you see the link between individual freedom and social responsibility as essentially mutually supported and sustained, then it is clear that the real threat to individual freedom comes from the denial of community and the challenges to freedom produced by the collapse of community.

In the end, those who have acquired, inherited, or built wealth cannot hire enough police to protect themselves and their property from a permanent and hopeless (as in without any hope of personal progress) underclass. Sitting comfortably in one's house in a gated or moated community in South Florida or Arizona, or in upstate New York, and, hearing of unrest among armies of regionally located perpetually unemployed and impoverished, leads one to contemplating, over martinis and canapés, whether the minimum-wage security guard at the gate would risk much to hold back an angry, hopeless, and dispossessed crowd. Not a pleasant contemplation. And even if one could do so in one's own neighborhood (the gated community) or country, which is unlikely, the global migratory patterns produced by joblessness are themselves uncontainable. And, even if they were containable, the interruptions to both the business cycle and financial system could cause those with assets meaningful losses. The importance of community is no luxury or Fabian prayer.

It is at the very essence of stability and freedom.

It is the true guarantor of the "order" in law and order.

It is at the very base of the moderate imperative.

10

Business and Government

It is endemic to much of the neoconservative view of a society and a world divided into competing interests that business and government be intrinsically opposed to each other.

Some of this emanates from a resentment that took root in business around the time of the New Deal in the U.S. when the bureaucracy doubled in size. Some harkens back to the anti-bureaucratic bias the "best and brightest" brought to John F. Kennedy's Washington in their enthusiasm to circumvent the "channels" and routines of the Eisenhower administration. Candidates for the presidency, from Wallace to Carter to Reagan to Clinton, have dined out shamelessly on the anti-Washington bias, and raised large campaign dollars from American business while doing so.

The distinction between Wall Street and Main Street, artfully developed by Ronald Reagan, gave a further dimension to the parsing of the forces of evil. Washington, in this lexicon, is the bureaucratic enemy; Wall Street, on occasion, is co-equal in the realm of ignoring the people's genuine interests; Main Street, on the other hand, the repository of all the virtues of small business, the Chamber of Commerce, and the like, is the last and only reliable metaphor for Mr. and Mrs. Average American. One can run for office to defend Main Street, but never to defend Wall Street or the bureaucracy. At least not in the U.S.

Yet, when the Gingrich Congress swept into power in 1994, and with the budgetary impasse contrived by the Contract with America crowd to close down large segments of the American federal government, Americans discovered that in thousands of towns and cities across the land, the bureaucracy was as much a part of Main Street as the Wal-Mart or the Dairy Queen. As laid-off workers in passport offices and post offices and the like could not pay their rent or make their mortgage payments or buy Christmas presents for their kids, and as supper-hour newscasters put the local faces and sounds of these local folk on the air, the perception of who was right and who was wrong began to shift meaningfully. This shift is credited by some with the reinvigoration of the Clinton presidency and his candidacy to succeed himself — the first Democrat to do so since the father of the New Deal himself, Franklin Delano Roosevelt.

Roosevelt grew the bureaucracy a couple of times, once during the New Deal and again during World War II.

Business was very much on board for the war effort, performing superbly and profiting meaningfully in the cause, despite their earlier hatred of the New Deal.

But it is significant that the one Democrat in half a century to be re-elected to the White House would get his key boost after a stunning midterm sag in the polls, from a neoconservative frontal attack on the bureaucracy — a bureaucracy he and most presidents since Eisenhower had run against.

In Canada there was no significant business angst about the bureaucracy until the confiscatory measures brought in by the 1968-1982 Trudeau Liberals through measures like the Foreign Investment Review Agency and the National Energy Program. Until those two events, and the MacEachen budget of 1991, business generally viewed government as an ally in the prewar and postwar years. Canada had no one at the turn of the century to attack the large single family or company, or multiple industry holdings in the way Teddy Roosevelt attacked the multi-industry trusts in the U.S. World War II saw a meaningful and cooperative effort in all areas of war production. There was no New Deal in Canada that threatened the underpinnings of Canadian enterprise, just incremental pieces of social policy that slowly constructed a safety net of some value.

In the growing 1950s, the Liberal St. Laurent government was, as a source of procurement, grand projects with public funds, pipeline permits, and the like, a great friend to large business, multinational business, and domestic and overseas suppliers.

When the post-1970s oil shocks, increasing safety net costs, and inflationary pressures produced growing needs for sovereign debt, Bay Street and Wall Street handled the requirement without any serious complaint about the policy's drift.

And while the excesses of C. D. Howe, a powerful and manipulative, if visionary Liberal minister of industry, in Canada may well have helped defeat the Liberals, on issues like the pipeline, there is little evidence that the public anger was related to anything more than Liberal arrogance and the crushing appeal in 1957-58 of the Tory "time for a change" battle cry.

The genuine antipathy between business and the Ottawa establishment emerged during the Trudeau years.

The Foreign Investment Review Agency had the effect of complicating intrinsic built-up value in a business or enterprise, especially when the putative purchaser or merger target or acquisition of a Canadian enterprise happened to be outside Canada. While their thresholds were relatively high and some approvals quite perfunctory, this agency in the Trudeau years was supposed to work in confidence respecting supplicant's proprietary information. Yet stories abounded that when companies were in play, FIRA would canvass prospective Canadian purchasers (often the companies most in local competition with the supplicant) to see if they would like to step in and purchase an asset that might otherwise be bought by the Germans or Americans or French. Having the regulatory capacity to ban a foreign investment, they could literally force a domestic disposition even to one's worst domestic competitor. If that is not confiscation, it is unclear what the word means.

And the National Energy Program was in many respects worse. It literally confiscated royalties and exploration sites and then taxed what was left. It composed a two-price system on western oil whereby the world bought oil from Alberta at the real price and the rest of Canada got it at a lower price. It depressed the prairie economy and angered just about every businessperson west of the Manitoba-Ontario border. And because of the permanent confiscatory elements of the policy and the arbitrary nature of its operation it produced a permanent and healthy suspicion on the part of Bay Street and Main Street relative to Ottawa's destructive capacity.

The 1981 Liberal Allan J. MacEachen federal budget (he was finance minister at the time) was, however, the coup de grace in terms of telling both Main Street and Bay Street just how out of touch with street level reality Ottawa had become. Huge mistakes were made on the tax measures, and issues relating to annuities, the status of real estate, and construction investment already started produced not only a backlash but also the embarrassing specter of government slinking back into the House of Commons to reverse its own budgetary provisions. From FIRA, business got a straight sense of how willful and manipulative Ottawa could be. From the NEP, business saw confiscatory excess it had not thought possible. From the 1981 budget, it saw just how incompetent and disconnected Ottawa, the bureaucracy, and the bureaucracy's party, the Liberals, could be — and were.

While they will likely claim different roots, the

truth is that many of the better pro-business and government lobby organizations, like the Fraser Institute, the Federation of Independent Business, and even the more established Business Council on National Issues, received major initiating gusts of wind in their sails during this period.

On both sides of the border, government is now seen by large segments of the business community as a source of capricious regulations and wrong-headed or destructive fiscal and social policy. There are exceptions, of course, as when President Reagan lowered taxes and boosted defence spending, or when Prime Minister Mulroney brought in free trade and did away with both FIRA and the NEP. But in general, the growth of lobbying actually can be traced by Canada to the confiscatory Liberal period of 1968-84 (especially from 1972 on) and in the United States to the Kennedy attack on steel. In both cases, it was not so much the bureaucracy that was leading the change as it was a willful president and prime minister, themselves a little disdainful or condescending about the bureaucracy. They imposed their egocentric policy whims on their countries.

◆

It would be hard from this history to justify anything other than eternal vigilance on the part of industry on either side of the 49th parallel.

How do they do business and avoid being used by neoconservative extremists to fund and encourage the kind of anti-community, anti-government bias that is, in and of itself, a threat to the stability and productivity of any society in which one is investing or contemplating an investment?

How does business — the engine of economic growth and a major part of society's raison d'etre — position itself on the spectrum of the issues of decision and community so clearly underlined in the battle against neoconservative excess?

The answer is both complex and simple. Complex because the men and women who make up the range of enterprise that runs from Main Street to Wall Street in the U.S. and Bay Street in Canada are citizens, voters, taxpayers, parents. They have views on these issues affected by each of the roles in their lives. It is complex as well because different businesses have different interests in terms of the size and scope of government — and the very nature of society itself.

It occurs to me that this very complexity and diversity is the compelling rationale for the simple answer. I offer a few rules:

(1) The business of business is business. As entities given licences and corporate letters patent, companies exist to fuse investment, innovative risk, hard work, and shareholder trust into profits for those shareholders, who may be pension funds, managers, public capital markets, or the nice woman next door. The business of business is business. When business decides otherwise, it is heading for trouble.

(2) Political parties, lobby groups, political advocacy foundations, and Political Action Committees have every right to exist, ply their wares, and seek corporate contributions. But these contributions should in no way be subsidized by the tax deductibility exemption. Private companies who feel so inclined, or public companies who can justify it to their shareholders, should feel free to give cash to any cause they favor in a free society. But if it is a political party, candidate for office, Political Action Committee, or political advocacy foundation, then that donation should be after tax, and, declared by the recipient publicly and *quarterly*, not a year and a half later.

(3) The corporation, however material and however transient, is in and of itself an expression of community. Shareholders (who could be retired

pensioners or mid-career teachers next door) are united in common enterprise and pervasive common interest with managers and employees (who may also be shareholders), with customers, suppliers, and sales agents across a region, state, country, continent, or planet. Their community of interest has a precise formative history, and they are constantly reinventing the entity they share to reflect modern, real market, and human reality.

As such, corporate and common interest in communities is a critical buttressing contributor to the quality of life of a company's stockholders and shareholders. The traditional conservative will to sustain community and stability is of great value to the corporate community. Buchanan-style divisive, polarizing, neoconservative attacks on institutional constructs, or the isolationist bias of some of neoconservatism, is ultimately a greater threat to the corporate community interest than much of the aimless chatter that comes from the left.

(4) However, while it is perhaps a little counterintuitive for some in business, disengaging from the ultimately destructive policies of the far right would provide a new, liberated opportunity to act in a nonpartisan way as a separate source of new ideas and fresh arguments around how one builds community in the future.

When business is deemed to be championing those partisan causes that only appear to be advancing their own narrow interests, they are and always will be suspect; however, business has every right to do so.

The opportunity here is to break free of partisan presumption and compartmentalization while still engaging on the issue of community in a creative and dynamic fashion, a community that has a meaningful impact on business — like infrastructure, education, health care, or crime prevention. And the opportunity here is to do so outside and away from the new right's nihilistic attack on all government and bureaucracy.

(5) The media have their job to do. Political parties and politicians have their job to do. Labor has its job to do. None is joined at the hip. None has any duty to each other to speak of, except common courtesy, that is in any way parallel to their duty to the public interest as they see it.

Corporate legitimacy comes from its economic performance, the accountability of its corporate leadership to the shareholder, and the competence with which it faces the larger world. Media legitimacy comes from integrity, economic viability, and interest, on occasion, in the unvarnished truth. Political legitimacy comes from seeking and being elected to public office for a fixed period of time. None of these lines of legitimacy intersect, however they may exist in the same universe and under similar conditions. But they are all separate spheres, and they need not merge or be headed in the same direction in a pluralist and open society.

Corporations who see themselves as supporters of the neocon process of social deconstruction limit their impact and undercut their influence. They may believe they are helping an anti-government crusade that cannot but help their own best interests.

In fact they are hostages to the kind of intellectually entrepreneurial advocates of excess that could just as easily be their undoing.

11

Of Nation and Enterprise

The challenge for traditional conservatives, whichever of the two mainstreams in North America they are a part, Republican or Progressive Conservative, is to define a cohesive economic and social framework for our time. The risk in not doing so is that the new right with its intellectual appeal to selfishness, with its elevation of greed to the status of a core freedom, with its use of fear and divisiveness, will build a beachhead that forever fractures the conservative mainstream. What we are left with is the perpetual election of Clintons and Chretiens and their (intellectual?) partisan heirs.

A conservative movement that is fragmented is of no greater value to the nation than one that is too narrow. It is the narrowness that produces the fragmentation; the fragmentation that gives licence to the narrowness. They feed on each other. Continued electoral defeat simply produces the core fragmentation that begins the downward spiral.

What happened to Republicans in 1992 spoke of a conservatism that had the virtues of moderation and decency in George Bush but seemed, no doubt unfairly, despite economic successes and the positive impact of the Gulf War, disconnected from the day-to-day life of Americans. The Perot phenomenon, and the voters his campaign stole from the Republican mainstream, made the most of that disconnect and elected Clinton, a "new democrat" who was more a democrat of the center than a democrat of the left that Americans had twice rejected for Ronald Reagan, and once for George Bush. The Republican fragmentation that followed produced the ascendancy of the new right through Gingrich in 1994. The core mistake of the class of '94 and of some Republican strategists was to be overtaken by their own propaganda and press clippings. They were not successful because of the Contract with America but in spite of it! They were the only vehicle available by which Americans could show displeasure with the Clinton administration. From the snafu on health care, Waco, budget dysfunction, anxieties over NAFTA, and the rest, there was no lack of national and regional reasons to express that disapproval. And one of the geniuses of the American system is the ability to send such a message through midterm elections, without changing the president or the partisan affiliation of the administration.

The congressional victory of 1994 produced a bubble mindset on the part of far too many Republicans amid the kind of ideologically based denial of nation the brand of conservatism in the Contract with America provided. And that produced a dynamic that moved too rapidly.

The Democrats' understanding of what happened in 1994 moved determinedly to respond to legitimate public anxiety and close the gap between the American people and their president. The Republicans, auto seduced by their own Gingrich-centered narrow neocon platform for 1994 and its alleged role in the electoral success of 1994, widened the gap between themselves and the American people.

It is as if they produced a universe within which to select a presidential candidate that reflected as little of America's electoral and public opinion mainstream as possible. One got the sense that the only reason the flat earth society could not find a candidate was that they could not adequately fund their own PAC. What one saw was:

Colin Powell, one bright shining link with U.S. mainstream aspirations and hope, ambushed by the purveyors of the narrowest of views.

Senator Phil Gramm boasting to a National Rifle Association convention about his mother's guns.

Pat Buchanan opposing women in military academies and using "cock your guns" as a rhetorical flourish.

Lamar Alexander, in his plaid shirt, calling for social services to be administered by the charitable sector.

And even decent people, like Bob Dole, having to come to terms with the Christian Coalition. (It was as if the Grand Old Party, utterly exhausted from the internal damage Gingrich's polices had done, reached to Dole as an honorable standard bearer to see themselves through.)

Gingrich, the great "prime ministerial" leader from Georgia, the architect of the Contract with America, was well hidden in 1996.

The Republicans had drifted away from the old Disraeli Tory balance and appeal implicit in Nation and Enterprise. They had become only Enterprise, leaving the entire ground underneath Nation for Mr. Clinton to espouse.

◆

In today's polemic, Nation and Enterprise speaks to the balance between economic imperatives on the one hand and the imperatives of the community, the country, the way we live together, on the other. If you desert any side of this balance you desert the only traditional conservative balance that reflects a broad and populist framework. When conservatives desert that balance they weaken their core and dilute their prospects — and almost always lose elections.

In Canada, the end of the Mulroney era, when he announced his resignation in early 1993, meant that the Progressive Conservatives had to remake a new version of the Nation and Enterprise framework for their party and country. The determined program of free trade, three unratified constitutional agreements, participation in the Gulf War, land settlement with the aboriginal population, tax reform, and new child tax benefits had held together two winning Conservative majorities in 1984 and 1988 — never before done since Canada's first prime minister, Sir John A. Macdonald. But this process, and the willful prime ministerial personality essential to making it happen, had reduced party support in the polls. In the wake of Mulroney's decision to step down, Conservatives had to sort out what the future meant for their coalition.

Every successful Conservative leader had built his own coalition in Canada around a contemporary version of Nation and Enterprise. William Davis and Peter Lougheed did in Ontario and Alberta in the 1970s and '80s. Robert Borden, R. B. Bennet, John Diefenbaker, and Brian Mulroney did so nationally. Robert Stanfield and Richard Hadfield did so in Nova Scotia and New Brunswick respectively, with Stanfield almost doing so at the national level.

The leader the Progressive Conservatives chose in 1993, the Right Honourable Kim Campbell, was unable either to articulate her own Nation and Enterprise framework or to build her own coalition in the country. There was a hurried and harried Alice in Wonderland sense about her, especially in the ensuing election campaign, a quality that made what was probably an unavoidable but respectable defeat into a complete collapse.

The mistake Progressive Conservatives made in 1993 in the leader they selected was not dissimilar in form to the misreading of the 1994 congressional elections by the Republican party.

There was never any polling, private or public, on the main thrust of the Mulroney program, or his government's budgets, or specific nation-building initiatives like the fixed link to Prince Edward Island or the Hibernia oil fields or the new helicopter or naval procurements for the armed forces indicating great public opposition to these steps lay just ahead. Public opposition was to the Mulroney style, to the willfulness and imperious quality attributed by his detractors to his prime ministerial activities. No one realized the impact of this more than Mulroney himself. Which is why, after having done all he could on the free trade, NAFTA, tax reform, and constitutional fronts to modernize the nation, increase productivity, and put Canadians on an even playing field with their global competitors — while preserving the safety net — he stepped aside, hoping to carry the unpopularity with him and away from the party.

Two months before he announced his resignation, the party was polling in single digits. The party moved up into the mid-30s upon his announcement, and when Kim Campbell was chosen leader she and the party enjoyed an approval rating unprecedented for any incumbent prime minister in three decades.

But the party had chosen a new style, the first female leader in Canada's history, the first from British Columbia, and the first true boomer generation leader, without having any idea of the substance of her views. In this last characteristic, they were at one with the candidate they had chosen. Canadian Progressive Conservatives had misunderstood what the public was saying. The public believed in and voted for the essential balance of the particular form of Nation and Enterprise between 1984 and 1992. They wanted a change in leadership, they wanted a change in emphasis. They did not want a desertion of Nation and Enterprise.

In fact, one only has to look at the Liberal government's popularity since election in 1993. While not without vulnerability, that popularity has been built on the largely avuncular and affected Forrest Gump persona of the Liberal prime minister and the precise if more intense continuation of the fiscal, economic, and trade policies of the previous government.

A change in style did not mean a surrender of the Nation and Enterprise framework. The Progressive Conservatives ended up surrendering both in some measure to the parties of the left and right, with the result that each of the delighted recipients poached their way to pieces of the national Tory constituency.

Until such time as Canadian Progressive Conservatives reclaim their own Nation and Enterprise constituency with a compelling philosophical and economic framework, they will be in a difficult fight for relevance. To be seduced by the siren call of the simplistic new right would be to permanently surrender the claim to be the Nation and Enterprise party Canadians chose to advance that cause.

And that cause, in both the United States and Canada, each in a way that reflects the separate cultural and historical evolution of the two countries, is simply the cause of an integrated view of society that leaves no one behind while liberating the forces of enterprise and productivity to generate wealth. It is a view that leaves aside the laissez faire liberalism of naive belief in the invisible hand or the perfectibility of human nature. It is a view that embraces order as the core product of fairness and law, and institutions that embody these values. It is that *order* which is the true and durable foundation of the compelling freedom that distinguishes a society of true opportunity and grace. It is the mix of freedom and order that sustains the will to community: to build it, sustain it, and advance it through a myriad of volunteer, personal, and humane activities across huge and disparate fields of interest.

And, Nation and Enterprise is intrinsically about the ability of forces of enterprise, of free markets, of investment, of fiscal balance and sanity to combine with the forces of fairness, humanity, and the community to build a compelling society of excellence and achievement. This is a society where the accident of one's birth does not determine the limitations of one's potential. Where the core values that sustain free enterprise also sustain equality of opportunity. Where the values that compel enterprise to seek more efficient and innovative paths also dismiss complacency about the state of society itself.

◆

No society can be stronger than its weakest link. No society premised on Nation and Enterprise can be complacent about undue constraints on enterprise. Nor can it be complacent about unfairness or insensitivity in its midst.

The politics of Nation and Enterprise engages as its true enemy division, selfishness, the politics of paranoia, and insensitivity — in other words, the core politics of too many in the neoconservative movement. The politics of recrimination and racial division; the politics of foxhole public policy and small-minded social retrenchment; the politics of class; the politics of huge economic protectionism, between neighborhoods, regions, provinces, states, urban and rural areas, white and black and native, different language groups. All this constitutes what the forces of the new right have embraced to advance their hierarchical view of society, where there are havens for them, and not much for anyone else.

For the new right to succeed it must destroy the mainstream conservatism of Nation and Enterprise; for the forces of Nation and Enterprise and for mainstream conservatism to advance through the broader instruments of the Progressive Conservative party in Canada and the GOP in the United States, they must confront the enemy of the new right.

While there may be compromise elsewhere, there can be no compromise on core balance implicit in Nation and Enterprise. Acceptance of that balance by all on the conservative side of the spectrum is the only basis, if ever, of a grand alliance on the center-right.

The protection of that balance can only come through the strength of will of the traditional conservative.

12

The Moderate Imperative

The core failure in the substance and tactics of the new right in both the United States and Canada is a fundamental misunderstanding of the reality of political power. Neoconservatives have in a sense become captives of their own propaganda. In the United States the modern postwar misuse of power was clearly embodied in the Kennedy presidency. And, as Garry Wills pointed out so persuasively in his 1982 work on the Kennedy family,* this misuse was tied to a notion of a ruling class, a political aristocracy that had the right in general to pursue

**The Kennedy Imprisonment: A Meditation on Power.* Little, Brown, Boston 1982.

initiatives only they would understand. This produced the disaster of the Bay of Pigs, the insane stratagems of what Dalton Camp has called a liberal-initiated war in Vietnam, the mindless assassination plots against Fidel Castro, and the massive pencil point risk of nuclear war over Soviet missiles in Cuba no more threatening or proximate than American missiles on Russia's border in Turkey.

But in terms of the raw use of executive order and decree, that general approach to power really set the American presidency apart in peacetime among all the democracies.

It is not surprising the new right, seeing the Kennedys and their use of power as the raw code of liberal might, would construct their own competing excess in the Congress, in lobby groups and think tanks, in intra-Republican party tests. It is about power. And power unused, the neocons' nostrums and direct mail wizards imply, is power to be seized by the other side.

So the way to ensure that the Republican party does not fall into dangerous moderate hands is by ambushing a Powell candidacy before it can translate broad public support into Republican delegates. The way to defend one version of fiscal integrity is to shut down the government.

In Canada, the Reform party has seen the departure of some of its more promising and thoughtful standard bearers and the election or re-election of Progressive Conservative majorities in Alberta and Manitoba. The stunning upset in favor of mainstream Progressive Conservatives in the provincial election in Ontario had more to do with Liberal voters who were far more focused on the Nation and Enterprise balance implied in previous successful Ontario Tory campaigns.

Reform's power in the federal election of 1993, achieved during a clear Progressive Conservative vacuum both in leadership and policy, emerged from the capacity to divide. Increasing anti-Quebec animosities in the west, encouraging intransigence on native land claims, feeding an anti-politician and anti-government cynicism, arguing for tougher law and order treatment of the most juvenile of criminals, doubting the appropriateness of liberal refugee policies, attacking equalization between rich and poor regions in the name of fiscal restraint — all these speak to the Reform party's attempt to maximize their gains from the power to divide.

But in the end they make the very same mistake as their new right American friends and mentors: they misunderstand the nature of power.

◆

Power in a democracy comes not from the ability to divide or even the ability to direct. Power in a democracy ultimately comes from the capacity to persuade, and be persuaded by, the essential moderation of the population as a whole.

The ability to persuade is based on trust, and trust is based on a clear and established practice of not abusing that trust. Using government to divide, using government to impose narrow fundamentalist biases, using government to encourage unfairness by sins of omission or commission is precisely such an abuse.

Leaders or putative leaders who encourage a retreat from moderation seek to bolster the legitimacy of their narrow views and purposes by seeing the population become as disengaged as they are from a balanced view. These are the leaders who work not to prevent crisis but to create it and expand upon it. They seek to leverage it for their own purposes rather than prevent it by true and fair-minded actions.

The moderate imperative explicitly provides that a democracy's only real power is power shared and used sparingly, and where possible not at all. The legitimacy of a public office holder or aspirant seeking to lead by building a shared consensus about common responsibilities to each other is more enduring than the opponent who seeks power by turning one demographically distinct voter group against another.

Conservatives who believe they can accomplish their work without the instruments and conventions of moderation desert the high ground of that key balance between Nation and Enterprise. They desert the great visceral appeal that conservatives offer to those who want order and stability in their family, personal, neighborhood, community, business, professional, and national lives. National leaders, like the Democrats under Kennedy or the Cold War extremists of the past, who see the clandestine undermining of those with different views as appropriate ways to advance the business and interests of the United States succeed and often produce the opposite result. Moderation is not the holy grail of public policy or public life. But it is the essence of both conservative legitimacy and the legitimacy of self-government itself. If government not only fails to strengthen the stability of one's many frames of reference but actually acts to destabilize as many as possible, then of what use or value is government overall?

Which explains the new right's onslaught against the moderate, the incremental, the expertly calibrated in public policy and the politics of policy. Moderation is no feeding ground for the extreme or unbalanced. Incrementalism is no place for the proponents of polarity or division.

Polarity in social and policy debate, discouragement, fear, heightened anguish, and paranoia need the rapid swings of a debate of extremes that ensures no middle ground is possible. It paints all compromise as weakness of the most morally reprehensible kind. Moderation is the enemy of division and insensitivity. It is the core enemy of those on the extreme left and the extreme right.

The extreme left has been constrained by a march of history that left the excesses of doctrinaire socialism and totalitarian Marxism behind to join fascism as ideas whose time had come and passed, deserted by publics who rejected the body count produced by extremism of any kind. The tyranny of the chronically politically correct, so similar in its intolerance to the narrow moral imperatives of the newcon extreme, will, one hopes, face similar and reasoned judgment.

But the new right has yet, in all its immoderate excess, to be confronted for the half truths, misstatements, and rabid oversimplifications that form the basis of its neoconservative march. That it has, despite its many insensitivities, attracted many on the right who are young, intellectually rigorous, and public minded is to its credit. That those new minions have failed to blunt its excesses, moderate its merchandising of division, or lift up its perspective speaks only to the seductive power of a comfortable intellectual life in the basement of social discourse, untroubled and uncaring about whatever unfairness or suffering may abound.

There is a viral effect to all this if it is not confronted. It can lead to spineless Democrats who want a victory for which no pandering is beyond imagination. It can lead in Canada to Liberals who do more to cut social programs than any Conservative government in Canadian history. It can lead to British Tory Eurosceptics who would rather see a vacuous Labour leader assume power than support a moderate Conservative prime minister. It can lead to the Reform party in Canada, the Reform party of Mr. Perot in the U.S. All speak to the victory of excess over moderation, of the politics of division over a unifying public policy.

The moderate imperative has never been more vital. Those at the extremes will argue against moderation, or dismiss it as dithering in the face of huge and tough challenges. They must stamp out that imperative if they are, largely unchecked, to dominate the day.

Which is why the moderate imperative must be defended by conservatives throughout North America, and their fellow citizens, at all costs.

13

The View from Here

Recent election results in the United States, the United Kingdom, and Canada point clearly to the corrosive impact on mainstream conservatism of self-indulgent extremism on the right. The Republican party fragmented around the immoderate conservatism of Pat Buchanan and Phil Gramm and the Christian Coalition. Not even the skills of a distinguished long-term servant of the party and America like Bob Dole could undo the excesses caused by the Republican platform and the fissure produced by that platform between the GOP and the American people.

In the United Kingdom, the extreme anti-European, right-wing Tories fractured the

Conservative campaign of John Major and clearly undercut the only asset the Tories had in that campaign: the broad economic progress Britain had experienced under Major's more moderate continuation of the progress earlier made under Prime Minister Margaret Thatcher. Not unrelated to the nativism and xenophobia of the Buchanan campaign in the presidential primaries, the approach of these Tories spoke to a little Britain, walled off, small-minded, and disconnected from its own regional neighbors and opportunities.

In Canada, the excesses of the neo right experienced the full bloom of anti-Quebec and implicitly anti-French bigotry that has always fueled large parts of Preston Manning's movement. While his far-right Reform party did not increase its popular vote and came up against major roadblocks in the most populated provinces of Ontario, Quebec, Nova Scotia, New Brunswick, Prince Edward Island, and Newfoundland, it did consolidate its vote in Alberta and British Columbia, obtaining the position of official opposition with a ten-seat gain over the last parliament. The mainstream Progressive Conservatives increased tenfold to official party status and twenty seats in the House from six provinces.

The saddest reality in Canada, however, is the way the Reform party's far right, anti-Quebec

TV campaign actually strengthened the sovereigntist vote in Quebec. After the TV debates, the Progressive Conservative leader, Jean Charest, experienced a stunning surge in support, especially in Quebec; the sovereigntist vote there began to decline rapidly as more and more Quebeckers who had voted Liberal and sovereigntist in the 1993 federal election moved to Charest's vigorous, impassioned, and impressive view of a new coalition for a nation-building federalism. The Reform party's response, consistent with its roots and approach from the very beginning, was to launch a television ad that put a red circle bar across the faces of all leaders from Quebec, including the Liberal prime minister, Jean Chretien, and Mr. Charest, along with sovereigntist leaders, implying that they were all the same because they were Quebeckers. This classic bit of televised demagoguery was accompanied by a voice-over which implied that the Quebec issue should be decided by more than just politicians from Quebec. The visual TV imagery was profoundly bigoted. Of course the Reformers claim the intent of the voice-over was only to elicit broader participation in the unity debate by more than Quebec leadership. The ad, evoking all the most negative aspects of tribalism often spawned by excessive neocon divisiveness, quickly reversed the sovereigntist vote slide in Quebec, polarizing Quebeckers once again and reducing the seat totals available for those parties seeking conciliatory mandates. This was divide and conquer at its very best. In its excess it probably helped re-elect a slight Liberal majority by forcing many Canadians who were repulsed by this approach to desert the Progressive Conservatives; these Canadians voted Liberal especially in balanced and moderate Ontario where that party took all but two of that province's 103 federal seats. They did so to crush Reform.

◆

What do mainstream Progressive Conservatives in Canada, Republicans in the United States, and Tories in the United Kingdom face today, given these results? Not so much a challenge of electoral strategy but a first-principles challenge about the purposes of society and government. After all, no electoral strategy can possibly overcome doubt about the underlying values of the political movement one is part of or doubt about that movement's core purposes and directions.

There is no core deficiency in the balance and purpose of traditional conservatism, which seeks a balance between enterprise and social responsibility, between personal freedom and social obligation.

G. K. Chesterton observed that Christianity had not been tried and found inadequate; it had been found too difficult and left untried. That truism relates dramatically to traditional, balanced conservative values and considerations. Traditional conservatism, like Christianity, implies a discipline of balances — a discipline of rigorous assessment of those things that matter, and a clear avoidance of the things that do not. In today's far right climate, it is not trendy to question that all and every consumer trend in politics is of equal merit. It is not trendy to suggest that those who are charging ahead because of the stability and opportunities of a free society owe some duty to those who are being left behind through no fault of their own. It is not terribly fashionable to believe in the role of duly elected and democratic government to reflect the common interest, the greater stability, and the counterbalance of order needed absolutely to anchor the benefits of freedom.

But such questioning is unavoidably and fundamentally necessary if free societies are to keep their bearings and avoid a period of serious decline.

This central question has been raised and addressed in a host of different ways over the years. In 1962, Michael Oakeshott, a British conservative philosopher of note, put the role of government as a stabilizing force this way: "Now, the disposition to be conservative in respect of politics reflects a quite different view of the activity of governing. The man of this disposition understands it to be the business of a government not to inflame passion and give it new objects to feed upon, but to inject into the activities of already too passionate men an ingredient of moderation; to restrain, to deflate, to pacify and to reconcile; not to stoke the fires of desire, but to damp them down. And all this, not because passion is vice and moderation virtue, but because moderation is indispensable if passionate men are to escape being locked into an encounter of mutual frustration."*

In this context it is absolutely clear that people like Buchanan, Gramm, Podhoretz, Manning, or Perot are not conservatives at all. They are simply radicals engaged in the polemics and rhetoric all radicals have always engaged in.

This is not a radicalism Edmund Burke or Adam Smith had much time for. Burke's view of the state embraced it as a partnership at the very center of civil society. In his inaugural address George Bush put it this way: "What is the end purpose of this economic growth? Is it just to be rich? What a shallow ambition. Is there really any satis-

*_Rationalism in Politics._ Barnes and Noble, New York 1962.

faction to be had in being the fattest country? What will they say of us, the Americans of the latter part of the twentieth century? That they were fat and happy? I hope not."

Mr. Bush's thousand points of light, a phrase that evoked the promise of the voluntary and community-based sector, was a way, more gentle than specific, to bridge the gap between the self-centered, greed-inspired ethos that had grown up under the Reagan presidency to reconnect American government and governing premises with the values of compassion and civility associated with the American people and the millions of volunteer activities that have always characterized American society.

A conservative view of society rejects utterly the view promoted by ideologues on the left that achievement and wealth creation can only come at the expense of social justice and equality of opportunity. But a conservative must also stand against those strains on the far right of the spectrum that would unalterably prove the ideologues on the far left not only right but resoundingly so. And an integrated view of society and government, their relationship to business, private life, and freedom, is essential here to knit together all the disparate pieces into an organic, humane vision. This integrity, where the realities of freedom, responsibility, civility, and enterprise come together with social justice and equality of opportunity, is what the extremists on the far right and far left are unable to offer.

Their constituencies are tied to piecemeal solutions that appeal only to segments of the population. They are prisoners of the politics of market segmentation, a politics that speaks necessarily to a strategy of divide and conquer. It is the common thread between Perot and Buchanan and Gingrich in America, Manning in Canada, and the Eurosceptics and the more narrow Europhobes in the Tory party in the United Kingdom.

◆

Mainstream conservatives can and should operate on a broader and more unifying level.

When he was clearly but tentatively exploring the Republican presidential nomination, Colin Powell spoke of the need to make room at the American table for more, not less, of the American population. His words were not a comment on the sterility of right-left debates. They were a call to generosity of spirit, a generosity that builds unity from diversity and seeks common cause against adversity.

In the end, conservatism writ large is about

community. It is about the things we all do to make life more noble and dignified for all. It is about governments and political systems that seek to enhance the self-respect and self-worth of all citizens. It is about a society where risk, achievement, and effort are rewarded without constraint in order to generate the incentives that expand the economic wealth necessary to sustain genuine equality of opportunity. It is about a sense of nation that excludes no one because of the economic station, ethnicity, or race to which they may have been born. It is about a sense of social cohesion and balance that values all contributions and sustains the civility that encourages all to contribute.

This mainstream conservatism is neither naive about crime and exploitation nor unprepared to act in defence of the nation's interest. It is a conservatism of human rights and pluralism, at home and abroad, one that welcomes dissent and open debate about the ends and means available and attainable by free and democratic societies. It is not a conservatism of hard ideologies or contractual fiscal nostrums. It is a conservatism of fiscal prudence, restrained but humane, and creative government, a conservatism that embraces both the necessity of enterprise and the imperative of social justice.

It is a governing and political framework of the

heart and not just the pocket book. It is an approach to politics that reaches out to all those who would contribute their skills and ideas and efforts in good faith. It is a conservatism that embraces diversity and choice as affirmations of the human condition. Traditional conservatism intuitively understands this: there can be no freedom without the order that emerges from genuine equality of opportunity and the civility it implies.

It is not an approach that invites or solicits confrontation. Nor is it one that creates division where it need not exist. Its primary role is to sustain the strengths of an organic and integrated society where the partnership of freedom and responsibility makes ever stronger the sinews of democracy and opportunity.

◆

To borrow a phrase from the Cold War, mainstream conservatives who believe in this kind of approach must engage in a focused program of eternal vigilance. The far right is well funded, bolstered by economic and religious interests that can produce delegates, homework, volunteer power, and the capacity to skew or overtake almost any open democratic process. The intensity of their excess breeds a willingness to both "do the windows" and the other necessary jobs of grass roots political organization.

Unless mainstream conservatives are prepared to respond in kind and engage at the local level, the policy level, in the media, and wherever political debate is joined, the sheer force of repeated far right nostrums may well carry the day. In the short term that will mean repeated liberal victories in the United States, Canada, and the United Kingdom. It will mean no firm conservative presence at the center of government. It will mean, if it continues, the disenfranchisement of moderate conservatives in both the United States and Canada and continued fractiousness within the British Conservative party.

Above all, it may well mean the damming up of dissent, of the politics of ideas, and the discourse of civility. Universal and extreme notions of state-ordained social and private morality will cohabit with the politics of class, privilege, and division. The edges between competing economic groups will harden. The splits between urban and rural, employed and unemployed, the inter-generationally wealthy and the inter-generationally poor will harden. Communities will spend more and more tax dollars on police because they have been encouraged to spend less and less on the truly needy. Inter-generational conflict will be expanded and encouraged by far right conservative ideologues. The ability of society or community to provide a warm and opportune environment for personal growth and advancement will diminish. Values around public education, health care, social service, and voluntarism will wither in the face of an expanded social motivation around the selfish and self-centered.

It is not only the quality of society that will diminish but the very quality of democracy itself. And that deterioration will reduce the quality of people prepared to enter public service at the appointed, elected, or civil service level. Gaps in income will be exalted as proof of individual victory and progress. Society will become an altogether more mean-spirited and closed place.

This is not the democratic conservative ideal. This is not what those who believe in a civil conservatism should be prepared to accept. The balances and fairness of civil conservatism need not be swallowed by the simplistic forces that speak to the dark side of fears, divisions, and those things that diminish the human spirit.

Life, society, human endeavor, and community are not about greed. They are about self-reliance and sharing. They are about building and contributing. They are about love, compassion, and the will to reach out to help others.

The freedoms and requirements of balanced conservatism reflect the order, responsibility, and civility essential to protect these purposes. These are purposes that go far beyond the limiting and diminishing attraction of greed.

◆

Greed is not to be confused with the legitimate and enthusiastic pursuit of personal gain, financial progress for oneself or one's family, or the focused search for excellence. Greed is, in its political expression, the single-minded isolation of one's own accumulative and consumer goals to the insensitive exclusion of all other competing interests or aspirations. It must exist on the platform of winner take all. It requires not just a monomaniacal and intolerant approach to competing economic interests but also a similarly disengaged approach to dissenting political views.

Greed appropriates the entire right wing of a political spectrum to one narrow view; it cannot put water in its wine or embrace compromise as a creative step ahead. Which is why extreme neoconservatives attack the moderate wings of the American Republican or Canadian Conservative parties. Creative compromise, so often associated with Republicans like Eisenhower, Rockefeller,

Kissinger, Bush, and Baker, and with British and Canadian Tories like Ted Heath, John Major, Peter Lougheed, Bill Davis, and Robert Stanfield, is the enemy of neoconservative predators, for whom any compromise or ambiguity dilutes the narrow ideological response. Compromise — a creative commitment to a public policy process that differentiates between varied responses on varied issues — is the enemy of the greed-based intellectual framework.

Conservatism embraces compromise because compromise creatively engages opposing interests, where possible, in common cause. One need not, as neoconservatives sometimes protest, surrender one's principles to effect compromise; one need only accept the radical proposition that others who share this democracy with you also have principles which they hold just as dearly. Bridges cannot always be built — but it is never wrong to try. Traditional conservatism prefers the building of bridges — as opposed to the digging of moats. Moats seem the appropriate engineering counterpoint for the politics of greed-based neoconservativism.

That kind of bridge-building conservatism is a conservatism of the democratic mainstream. It is one that seeks to close the gaps between rich and poor, black and white, north and south, old and young, public and private. It is about a powerful will to enhance freedom and equality of opportunity by expanding the economic mainstream to include those who would, were it up to the ideologues of winner take all, otherwise be simply forgotten.

Setting aside the winner-take-all approach does not mean a philosophy or economy that has no worries. Quite the contrary. Winners must be celebrated and encouraged as constructive and driving forces that help energize a society. But the celebration of success does not license the denial of failure.

The reality of failure — where people are left behind through no fault of their own or where entire groups of citizens are unable to break into the economic mainstream — cannot be excluded from a holistic conservative framework for society.

And it is society as a whole that is the focus of a politics that goes beyond greed. There is a compelling conservative view of community, compassion, cohesiveness, and inclusion that is the essence of a politics of opportunity.

The politics of greed and the politics of opportunity are mutually exclusive. They are vastly different in purpose, process, and results.

When conservatives are focused on the politics of opportunity — and on equality of opportunity in particular — they tend to be on a rising tide of relevance and political influence. When they retreat to the divisive politics of exclusion, class, and nativism — implicit in the politics of greed — they disconnect from the economic and social mainstream and inherit the political whirlwind of sustained irrelevance.

Retreating to the politics of greed is an abdication of one's duty to the politics of opportunity and its capacity to liberate individuals, social groups, and communities.

The answer for conservatives is to reach beyond the narrow, beyond the small-minded, beyond the politics of insensitivity and envy. Above all, the answer for mainstream conservatism, in defiance of the siren call of extreme and simplistic solutions, pernicious and exclusionary policies, is to commit itself always to looking well beyond greed.

The politics of greed and a society based on that politics is no politics or society at all. Which should trouble not only mainstream conservatives but all citizens of democracies where hope, confidence, freedom, and opportunity truly matter.

Index